S0-BRJ-656

# The Scoop on What to Eat
## *What You Should Know About Diet and Nutrition*

ISSUES IN FOCUS TODAY

**Kathlyn Gay**

**Enslow Publishers, Inc.**
40 Industrial Road
Box 398
Berkeley Heights, NJ 07922
USA

http://www.enslow.com

*To Nissa Beth, who shares her enthusiasm for and knowledge about good health with her family and friends and through her California fitness studio.*

**Library of Congress Cataloging-in-Publication Data**

Gay, Kathlyn.
    The scoop on what to eat : what you should know about diet and nutrition / Kathlyn Gay.
        p. cm. — (Issues in focus today)
    Includes bibliographical references and index.
    Summary: "Discusses diet and nutrition for young people, including ideas for a well-balanced diet, good and bad foods to eat, the importance of exercise, and eating disorders"—Provided by publisher.
    ISBN-13: 978-0-7660-3066-4
    ISBN-10: 0-7660-3066-0
    1. Nutrition—Juvenile literature.  I. Title.
    RA784.G39 2009
    613.2—dc22                                        2008040382

Printed in the United States of America

10 9 8 7 6 5 4 3 2 1

**To Our Readers:** We have done our best to make sure all Internet addresses in this book were active and appropriate when we went to press. However, the author and the publisher have no control over and assume no liability for the material available on those Internet sites or on other Web sites they may link to. Any comments or suggestions can be sent by e-mail to comments@enslow.com or to the address on the back cover.

♻ Enslow Publishers, Inc., is committed to printing our books on recycled paper. The paper in every book contains 10% to 30% post-consumer waste (PCW). The cover board on the outside of each book contains 100% PCW. Our goal is to do our part to help young people and the environment too!

**Illustration Credits:** AP/Wide World, pp. 69, 87, 103; BananaStock, p. 46; Photos.com, pp. 1, 3, 5, 12, 30, 79 (upper right and lower left), 89; Shutterstock, pp. 3, 17, 23, 26, 34, 42, 52, 57, 61, 63, 73, 79 (upper left and lower right), 81, 94, 95, 97, 99, 101; U.S. Department of Agriculture, pp. 40, 53.

**Cover Illustration:** iStockphoto (large photo); U.S. Department of Agriculture (background); BananaStock (small inset photo).

# Contents

## Family, Friends and Food

If you are a sports fan—whether it is football, baseball, hockey, or basketball—one part of enjoying the game as a spectator usually means hailing a vendor for refreshments.

If you like video games, you and your friends may gather to compete—and indulge in snacks and drinks.

If you go to a movie at a theater with friends or family, you might snack on a large tub or bucket of popcorn.

If you take part in or attend a school graduation, you may go to a congratulatory dinner, a picnic for graduates, or other food-based event.

If you like to meet with classmates or friends after the school day is over, you may join your group at a favorite pizza or other fast-food place.

If you are invited to a birthday party, you, like most guests, will probably expect part of the festivities to include cake, ice cream, and a soft drink.

Whenever and wherever teenagers (or for that matter any group of people) gather, food and beverages are likely to be consumed. "Interaction over food is the single most important feature of socializing," according to anthropologist Sidney Mintz, at Johns Hopkins University. "The food becomes the carriage that conveys feelings back and forth."[1]

The old saying "Eat, drink, and be merry" often rings true on social occasions. But numerous experts on food and nutrition have some words of caution: Have fun, but be aware that some foods and beverages do little or nothing for your health and could even be harmful. For example, people are often tempted to eat and drink more than they need or really want when they socialize. If a person overeats too often, she or he may gain unwanted pounds. Here is how Professor Brian Wansink of Cornell University and the U.S. Department of Agriculture describes it:

> One of life's greatest pleasures is to share food with family and friends. What we don't always realize is how strongly our family and friends influence what we eat. When we're with people we enjoy, we often lose track of how much we're eating. We eat longer than we otherwise would, and we let others set the pace for how fast and how much we eat. . . . When we're with people we like, we tend to eat for longer than when we're by ourselves. . . . On average, if you eat with one other person, you'll eat about 35 percent more than you otherwise would. If you eat with a group of seven or more, you'll eat nearly twice as much—96 percent more—than you would if you were eating alone.[2]

Besides the social issue, it is common for many Americans to eat more than usual when they are stressed or unhappy.

Other behavioral, economic, and cultural factors related to food may lead to diverse health problems.

## Why Worry?

News stories, magazine features, and TV commentaries over the past two decades have made it clear that Americans are fatter than most other populations in the world. "The prevalence of overweight and obesity has increased sharply for both adults and children," according to the U.S. Centers for Disease Control and Prevention (CDC). For young people aged 12–19 years, the prevalence of overweight and obesity increased from nearly 11 percent in the period 1988–1994 to 17.4 percent in a 2003–2004 survey.[3]

The National Institutes of Health defines overweight as

> an excess of body weight compared to set standards. The excess weight may come from muscle, bone, fat, and/or body water. Obesity refers specifically to having an abnormally high proportion of body fat. A person can be overweight without being obese, as in the example of a bodybuilder or other athlete who has a lot of muscle.[4]

The CDC notes that overweight and obesity "are both labels for ranges of weight that are greater than what is generally considered healthy for a given height. The terms also identify ranges of weight that have been shown to increase the likelihood of certain diseases and other health problems."[5]

In some cases, a physician may diagnose a person as having a medical condition known as morbid obesity. This means the person is severely obese—one hundred pounds or more over the ideal body weight. Such a person is at great risk of obesity-related health conditions or serious diseases.

## BMI Calculations

The most commonly used method to calculate overweight and obesity is the body mass index (BMI). Adults may use a table showing height in inches along a vertical column and weight in pounds across a horizontal column. The BMI is indicated at the top of the table.

However, standard BMI tables for children and teenagers are different from those used by adults because as children grow their proportion of fat weight changes. It may be high at age eleven but lower at age thirteen as they grow taller. Thus when determining BMI for children and teenagers, health care professionals may use what are frequently called BMI-for-age charts.

Curved lines on a chart show percentiles, values on a scale of 100. A person's BMI plotted on the chart indicates whether her or his BMI exceeds or equals others of the same age and gender. If a ten-year-old girl is in the 50th percentile, this means that 50 percent of girls of the same age have a lower BMI. A sixteen-year-old boy might be in the 60th percentile, so 60 percent of boys of the same age have a lower BMI. Both female and male young people are considered overweight if their BMI is in the 95th percentile or higher.

The increasing BMI rates of Americans have raised health concerns. Being overweight or obese boosts the risk of having many diseases and adverse health conditions, including (but not limited to) diabetes, heart disease, stroke, arthritis, and some cancers. Severe obesity can "cause respiratory problems," according to doctors at the Medical College of Wisconsin. The physicians say, "Breathing is difficult as the lungs are decreased in size, and the chest wall is very heavy and difficult to lift. Daily activities such as shopping, yard work, stair climbing and exercise may be hindered by breathing problems."[6]

## Other Reasons for Concern

Many teenagers face eating disorders—destructive behaviors to lose weight that can lead to serious illnesses and sometimes even death. In addition, fad diets and controversial detox diet plans designed to rid the body of any toxic materials may impact one's

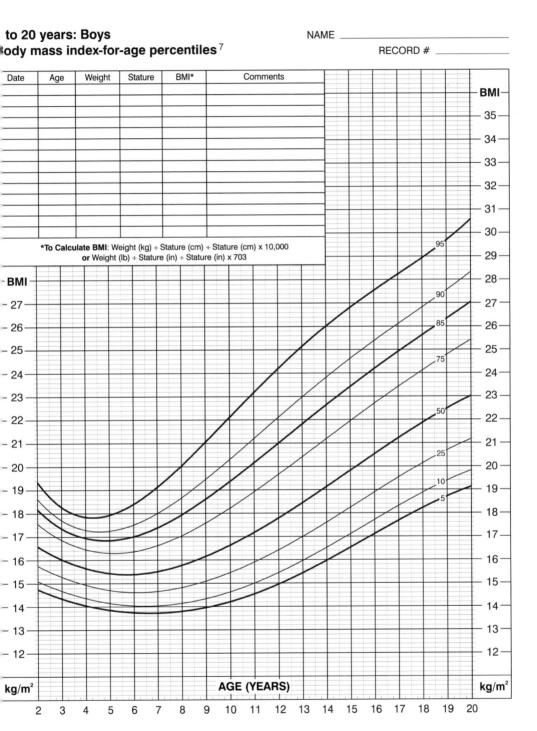

to 20 years: Boys
ody mass index-for-age percentiles [7]

NAME _____

RECORD # _____

**This chart can be used to monitor BMI for boys.**

According to the CDC, "The prevalence of overweight and obesity has increased sharply for both adults and children."

health in an adverse way, no matter what advertisements say about the benefits.

Questions also arise about eating out or buying carryout foods; are these practices good for a person's health? And who has not heard about "junk food" and "fast food"—are they the same thing and are they unhealthy? Are packaged convenience meals healthy?

Whatever types of meals people eat, it is important to know whether they are nutritious, providing the vitamins, minerals, protein, and other nutrients the body needs. Why? One teen, Allison Guthrie, has a response. She warned in *Teen Voices*:

> Unhealthy nutrition habits don't disappear when you get older. In fact, your current eating habits can determine the way you may eat later in life—and those habits can be hard to break! If you are 14 years old with a sky-high cholesterol level and you think you can just start over when you're older, think again. If teens don't take this issue seriously then we could have some major problems in our future.[8]

## Looking for the Positive

Besides the cautionary words, chapters in this book cover positive approaches. For example, some teens and adults—admittedly a minority—follow a vegetarian or semi-vegetarian regimen and consider it not only healthy but also enjoyable.

Maybe you are hesitant to try healthy foods because the word "healthy" makes you think of broccoli, brussels sprouts, spinach, or other vegetables with a reputation for being "good for you" but not particularly tasty. Well, think again. There are ideas for delicious and healthy items such as fruit smoothies, breakfast burritos made with whole-wheat tortillas, baked corn chips with mango salsa or black bean dip, veggie pizza, and apple slices with peanut butter and raisins. Numerous healthy choices are increasingly available in grocery stores, vending machines, and school cafeterias.

Finally, to be in top form, there are suggestions included in this book for a nutritious, healthy eating plan. But first it is important to know what kind of foods do little to improve health and what kinds provide the nutrients your body needs to function properly.

## Junk Food, Fast Food, Smart Food

*Junk food* is a term that has been bandied about a lot in recent years. One definition of junk food is any food or beverage that provides excess calories, fat, and salt and has little nutrient value. Such foods include snacks like high-fat potato chips, many fried foods, and candy bars. Sugary beverages are in the junk food category as well. They do not contain fat but are high in "empty calories"—calories that do not provide any nutrients. These foods make up one third of U.S. diets, according to a study by Gladys Block, professor of epidemiology and public health nutrition, University of California, Berkeley.[1] Nevertheless, not every bit of junk food has to be eliminated from one's diet. Small portions of snacks every now and then are not detrimental if the rest of your daily diet is nutritious and healthy—and you exercise to keep your weight in balance.

## The Fast Food–Junk Food Connection

Frequently the term *fast food* is used to mean junk food, but fast food and junk food are not necessarily the same thing. For example, some fast foods could be healthy choices, such as packaged salads found at restaurants like McDonald's and Wendy's. Another fast-food item is pizza, which is not necessarily unhealthy. Nutritionist Elaine Magee, who writes for WebMD, says that pizza can add nutrients "like cheese and tomato sauce" to the diet. "Add whole-wheat or part whole-wheat crust, plus veggies as a topping, and I'd say pizza completely exits the junk food category."[2]

On the other hand, some quick, convenient items like french fries or sugary soft drinks in fast-food restaurants could be categorized as junk food. "It's extremely difficult to eat in a healthy way at a fast-food restaurant. Despite some of their recent healthful offerings, the menus still tend to include foods high in fat, sugar, and calories and low in fiber and nutrients," cautions Mark Pereira at the University of Minnesota, lead author of a study published in the January 1, 2005, issue of the *Lancet*, a medical journal.[3] The study concludes that young adults who eat fast food more than twice per week gain more weight and have a greater increase in insulin resistance, which leads to diabetes, than those who eat such food less than once per week.

Although it is tempting to eat high-fat and sugary foods in fast-food restaurants, some people try to choose healthy items. One such person is teenager Marcus Howard, who told *Advertising Age* that he eats regularly at

**One definition of junk food is any food or beverage that provides excess calories, fat, and salt and has little nutrient value.**

McDonald's, and his "favorite thing there is Chicken Selects. I don't pay attention to the issue of healthy eating on a worldwide scale, but I pay attention to it for myself. I try to eat healthy, and other teens are also conscious about this."[4]

Chicken Selects, which are chicken-breast strips, could be a fairly healthy selection, but if calories are an issue, it depends on how many pieces are ordered. Three pieces contain 380 calories. There are 630 calories in five pieces, and 1,270 in ten pieces.[5]

Although fast-food restaurants offer plenty of items with low nutritional value, some chains like McDonald's, Subway, Taco Bell, Wendy's, KFC (Kentucky Fried Chicken), and others also offer foods low in sugar, fat, and calories and high in nutrients. Some menus even indicate the grams of fat and number of calories in meals. In addition, fast-food chains list the nutrients, fat, and calories of many of their popular items on their Web sites.[6]

McDonald's Web site chart, for example, shows that a 3.5 ounce hamburger contains 250 calories and 9 grams of fat. In comparison, a Big Mac has 540 calories and 29 grams of fat.

Burger King offers a healthier option to french fries—Apple Fries. These are slices of chilled fresh apples cut and served in a fries cup. Apple Fries contain 35 calories compared to 230 calories in a small order of french fries. The chain also serves unsweetened applesauce, Veggie Burgers, salads, and grilled chicken sandwiches.

While fast foods for the most part are *not* the best source of nutrition, they can fit into a healthy diet. The trick is to make smart choices whether eating out, at home, or on the school campus.

## Smart Food

There is no precise definition for smart food, although for this book the expression refers to foods and beverages that help the body function in a healthy manner. Such foods contain essential nutrients, chemical substances that are absolutely necessary for our bodies to function effectively. We have to depend on nutrients in our diet because our bodies are not able to produce many of them or cannot produce them in adequate amounts. Basic nutrients include proteins, carbohydrates, fats and oils, minerals, vitamins, and water. Although it may seem strange to consider water a nutrient, it is a nourishing substance that is vital for life.

According to the CDC:

> Research shows that good nutrition can help to lower people's risk for many chronic diseases, including heart disease, stroke, some cancers, diabetes, and osteoporosis [a disease that makes bones fragile and likely to break]. However, a large gap remains between healthy dietary patterns and what Americans actually eat.[7]

*Proteins.* Proteins are important nutrients and have numerous functions in the body. Primarily they build and repair body tissues, from hair and skin to bones and muscles. They also form antibodies that help fight infections. A protein called hemoglobin carries oxygen in the blood to every part of your body. The National Institute of General Medical Sciences calls proteins the "body's worker molecules" needed for "virtually every activity in your body."[8]

Proteins are made from bead-like strings of molecules called amino acids that come in many shapes and sizes. These amino acids can make thousands of different proteins, but scientists have determined that twenty-two of them are essential for good health. The body makes thirteen of these amino acids, but the other nine must come from food.

In the United States, the main source of protein is meat, with beef at the top of the list. Pork and poultry are other major protein sources. Dairy foods, fish, and eggs provide protein, as do grains, beans, nuts, and seeds. Along with beans, other vegetables also contain some protein, including broccoli, cauliflower, carrots, corn, garlic, and mushrooms.

*Carbohydrates.* Carbohydrates (or carbs for short) provide most of the energy our bodies need and all of the energy our brains need. Carbohydrates are made up of carbon, oxygen, and hydrogen; they combine to make sugar molecules, and come in two types, simple and complex carbohydrates.

Simple carbohydrates consist of one or two sugar molecules, while complex carbohydrates are made of long chains of sugar molecules and are usually called starches. The body metabolizes (breaks down) the sugar molecules in food to produce glucose, or blood sugar, which creates energy for cells, tissues, and organs. Simple carbohydrates, such as those found in fruit and milk, break down quickly and provide a burst of energy. But the blood glucose can drop quickly also, and a person may feel hungry or tired within a short time. Complex carbohydrates, which are found in foods like breads and cereals, rice, and legumes (beans, peas, and lentils), break down more slowly and provide energy over a longer period of time.

*Fats.* Fats are made up of chemical compounds called fatty acids (fats and fatty acids essentially mean the same thing). They have gotten a bad reputation over the past few decades as health experts and food advertisers have warned that too much fat is a health risk. Fatty acids also play a major role in cholesterol levels.

Cholesterol is a soft, waxy substance that our bodies make naturally, manufacturing it in the liver, and it also comes from animal products (meat, fish, and dairy foods) that we eat. Plant foods have no cholesterol. Cholesterol is transported in the blood to be used for normal body functions, including the production of hormones and vitamin D.

Cholesterol combines with protein and fatty acids to form high-density lipoproteins (HDL) and low-density lipoproteins (LDL). LDL, often called the "bad" cholesterol, can stick together to form plaque deposits on the walls of a person's blood vessels, leading to atherosclerosis, or blocked arteries. HDLs remove used cholesterol from the cells of the body.

Certainly, fats are not all bad. They help the body function properly—they are an energy source (fuel) and are used to produce cell membranes. Fats are also important for healthy hair and skin, provide flavor to foods, help you feel full, and are a source of calories, or energy units in food. Packaged foods and beverages have Nutrition Facts labels that show the calories per

**Depending on the ingredients, pizza can be an example of a "smart" fast food.**

serving and the amount of calories from fat. Serving sizes differ depending on the food or beverage. For example, a serving could be a cup of cereal, a slice of bread, an eight-ounce glass of juice, a tablespoon of mayonnaise, or ten crackers or chips. A label might show that a serving contains 60 calories, with 15 of those calories from fat.

According to U.S. dietary guidelines, people should consume no more than 30 percent of their calories from fat based on a daily diet total of 2,000 calories. But labels may not show percentages of fat in various foods. To determine the percentage of calories from fat, divide the number of calories from fat by the total calories and then multiply by 100. Using the total of 60 calories with 15 calories from fat, divide 15 by 60 and multiply by 100. The result is 25 percent of calories from fat.

Whatever the percentages, a study by the Harvard School of Public Health found that "the total amount of fat in the diet, whether high or low, isn't really linked with disease. What really matters is the *type of fat* in the diet."[9]

There are four main types of fatty acids: saturated, monounsaturated, polyunsaturated, and trans. The U.S. Food and Drug Administration (FDA) explains:

> All fatty acids are chains of carbon atoms with hydrogen atoms attached to the carbon atoms. A saturated fatty acid has the maximum possible number of hydrogen atoms attached to every carbon atom. It is therefore said to be "saturated" with hydrogen atoms, and all of the carbons are attached to each other with single bonds.[10]

Saturated fats are solid at room temperature, and they can be found in food from animals such as lard, butter, cheeses, and other dairy products. They can increase the risk for various diseases, including heart disease. Unsaturated fats—monounsaturated and polyunsaturated—have fewer hydrogen atoms attached and are found in liquid vegetable oils and fish; they reduce heart disease risks.

## Where the Calories Are

Calories are not limited to those in fat. They are also found in carbohydrates and protein in food. On the nutrition label, the amounts of nutrients like fat, carbohydrates, and protein are shown in grams. One gram is about 1/5 teaspoon. It takes about five grams to equal a teaspoon.

To determine the total amount of calories in a food serving, check the label again. Near the bottom of most labels is the calorie equivalent for carbohydrates, protein, and fat. There are only 4 calories per gram of protein and 4 calories per gram of carbohydrates, while food fat contains 9 calories per gram. The higher amount of calories in fat is one reason for warnings against high-fat food. Suppose the label on a loaf of bread states that one slice (a serving size) has 10 grams of carbohydrates, 2 grams of protein, and one gram of fat. To compute the total calories in the slice of bread, multiply the 10 grams of carbohydrates by 4 calories (per gram), which equals 40 calories. Multiply the 2 grams of protein by 4, and the result is 8 calories. The one gram of fat multiplied by 9 equals 9 calories. To find the total calories add 40 + 8 + 9 = 57. Thus the 57 calories in one slice of bread are part of the daily total based on a 2,000-calorie diet.

Not everyone needs the same number of calories for good health, however. A teenager playing school sports may need 3,000 to 3,500 calories a day, but a less active person may require less than 2,000. When people take in more calories than they burn, they gain weight; they lose weight when they consume fewer calories than they use.

Another type of fat is trans fat, which naturally occurs in small amounts in butter, milk products, cheese, and meats. But trans fats are also formed when liquid oils are made into solid fats like shortening and solid margarine. To produce trans fat, hydrogen is added to vegetable oil. The process, called hydrogenation, increases the shelf life and flavor of foods. However, trans fat also acts like saturated fat and boosts the LDL or "bad" cholesterol in the blood.

As of January 2006, the FDA required food manufacturers

to list the amount of trans fat on nutrition labels, and some cities and counties have banned trans fats in restaurant meals, some delis, and bakeries—New York, Philadelphia, and Baltimore, Maryland, are examples. In 2007, Montgomery County, Maryland, became the first in the nation to ban trans fat in supermarket bakeries and delis, according to a report in the *Washington Post*.[11] Other communities are proposing such bans.

To comply with bans and the FDA ruling, some snack manufacturers have switched to unsaturated fats such as canola (made from rapeseed), sunflower, soybean, or corn oil. A variety of restaurants serving fried foods have also replaced saturated fats with the unsaturated kind. For one, Kentucky Fried Chicken uses unhydrogenated soybean oil, and in May 2008 McDonald's announced that it had eliminated trans fat in its cooking oil.[12] But according to *U.S. News & World Report*, makers of baked goods are not making the transition as easily because solid fats like shortenings give cakes, donuts, and other items "their light texture and flakiness as well as the rich flavor." Some no longer use trans fats but instead use palm oil or palm kernel oil, which are saturated fats.[13]

Fats essential for body functions include omega-3 fatty acids, also known as polyunsaturated fatty acids. Omega-3s are essential for brain function as well as for normal growth and development, and may help reduce "the risk of heart attack, dangerous abnormal heart rhythms, and strokes in people with known cardiovascular disease," according to the National Library of Medicine and the National Institutes of Health.[14] These fatty acids also slow the buildup of plaque in the arteries and slightly lower blood pressure, helping to prevent strokes.

The body does not produce these fats, so they must be ingested from such foods as fatty fish (salmon, albacore tuna, sardines, and lake trout are examples), flaxseed, walnuts, canola oil, and unhydrogenated soybean oil. The American Heart

Association (AHA) recommends "eating fish (particularly fatty fish) at least two times a week. Fish is a good source of protein and doesn't have the high saturated fat that fatty meat products do."[15] Yet nearly all fish and shellfish contain mercury, a toxin. For most people this is not a health problem. But the U.S. Environmental Protection Agency and the Food and Drug Administration issued a warning in 2004 that young children, pregnant women, and nursing mothers should avoid some types of fish with high levels of mercury, such as shark, albacore (a type of tuna), swordfish, and king mackerel. Instead, the government agencies recommend eating fish and shellfish low in mercury levels, including canned light tuna, shrimp, pollack, and catfish.[16]

*Vitamins and minerals.* To assure good health, vitamins and minerals are important components in the diet. These are micronutrients, meaning they are needed only in small amounts. But those small amounts help the body grow and develop normally and function properly.

For example, calcium is a mineral required for the development of strong bones. The body cannot produce calcium, so it must be absorbed through foods rich in calcium such as milk, yogurt, and green leafy vegetables. Vitamin D aids in the calcium absorption process. Sometimes called the "sunshine vitamin," vitamin D can be made by the body after exposure to the sun. Some fish are good sources of vitamin D and small amounts can be found in beef liver, cheese, and egg yolks. Fortified foods, those with added nutrients, provide most of the vitamin D in the U.S. diet. Milk is an example. Ready-to-eat breakfast cereals often contain added vitamin D, as do some brands of orange juice, yogurt, and margarine.

Along with vitamin D, other needed vitamins include A, several B vitamins, C, E, and K. Here is a brief list of what these vitamins do and what food sources provide them:

- Vitamin A helps in the formation and maintenance of healthy teeth, bones, and skin; it also promotes good vision. Vitamin A food sources include lean meats, dairy foods, green and yellow vegetables, and fruits with beta carotene, which converts to vitamin A in the body.

- B vitamins are important for metabolism—the processes within the body that create and use energy. Whole grains, lean meats, poultry, fish, and dairy products are some good sources of B vitamins.

- Vitamin C promotes healthy teeth and gums, helps the body absorb iron, and aids in healing wounds. Citrus fruits, tomatoes, and green vegetables are some foods that provide vitamin C.

- Vitamin E assists in the production of red blood cells. Vegetable oils, nuts, seeds, and green vegetables are some foods that contain vitamin E.

- Vitamin K is important as a coagulant—it helps stop bleeding after an injury or a nosebleed. Food sources include cabbage, cauliflower, and leafy green vegetables.

Calcium is just one of more than a dozen minerals our bodies need. Others are iodine, iron, magnesium, phosphorus, potassium, selenium, and zinc. These are their functions and food sources:

- Iodine is used by the thyroid gland to produce hormones, and it aids in growth.

- Iron is essential for the formation of hemoglobin, which carries oxygen to cells, and it helps prevent anemia. Some food sources are red meats, fish, eggs, and leafy green vegetables.

Donuts are full of "empty" calories—because of the high sugar and fat content, very little nutrition is provided.

- Magnesium provides numerous metabolic functions and is needed for normal bone growth and healthy nervous system. Whole grains, leafy green vegetables, nuts, beans, bananas, and apricots are some foods that contain magnesium.

- Phosphorus aids in blood clotting, bone and teeth formation, cell growth, contraction of the heart muscle, normal heart rhythm, and kidney function; assists the body in the utilization of vitamins and the conversion of food into energy; and is involved in virtually all physiological chemical reactions.

- Potassium is an important electrolyte in the blood that is needed for a healthy nervous system and helps regulate blood pressure and the proper functioning of the heart and liver. Most foods contain some potassium, but bananas, oranges, orange juice, and dried fruits are especially good sources.

- Selenium helps fight cell damage and is needed to maintain the immune system. Sources include fish, shellfish, red meat, liver, chicken, and eggs.

- Zinc helps keep the immune system functioning and is needed for cell division, growth, and healing of wounds. Oysters and other seafood, meat, eggs, and whole wheat products are some food sources of zinc.

Water or other liquids in the diet keep us alive. We can survive for weeks without food but only a few days without fluid intake. All of the body's cells and organs depend on water to function. Water helps to transport foods through the intestinal tract and to eliminate waste. It is a lubricant that helps protect joints, and it regulates body temperature.

Our bodies do not store excess water, so our daily diet

should include enough water to maintain good health. A common question is: How much water does a person need? The usual answer has been at least eight glasses of water daily. But in recent years, health experts say a variety of beverages help supply the fluids the body needs. Most fluids come from water, milk, juice, soup, coffee, tea, and other beverages. About 20 percent of water comes from the food we eat, especially fruits and vegetables.

In addition, water needs depend on a person's age, physical activity, and exposure to heat. For example, people can lose water through perspiration during strenuous physical activity in hot weather and would need to increase their daily fluid intake. For most people, thirst is the guide that determines whether to drink water or other beverage.

Clearly, making smart choices in foods and beverages involves some knowledge about nutrients, which, as described earlier, can be complex and sometimes difficult to determine. But the work may be done for you under certain circumstances: Healthy snacks and drinks may replace junk food in vending machines, and restaurant menus may highlight healthy items. In the school cafeteria, nutritious meals and beverages are offered, although some students opt for school snack bar foods, such as high-fat hot dogs and sugary sodas. For meals prepared at home, fresh and packaged food choices can be based on the USDA MyPyramid. Guidelines or plans established by medical organizations such as the Mayo Clinic, the National Institutes of Health, and WebMd or by nutritionists and dietitians also help with healthy meal preparation.

There are many campaigns under way to educate Americans about "smart" foods and beverages that can improve health. It is also important to know why and how we eat in order to avoid situations that prompt us to overindulge, gain weight, and consume unhealthy foods.

# Why and How We Eat

Obviously, we eat because we are hungry and need food as fuel for survival. But there are other reasons we consume certain foods and beverages. Sometimes it is to relieve stress or to calm emotions. Other times we eat simply because people around us are doing so. Suppose you had a hearty breakfast, but someone among your family or friends has a box of fresh donuts and invites you to indulge. You are not hungry, but you eat a donut (or maybe two or three) anyway.

Being around food—seeing and smelling it—can prompt a person to eat even though she or he feels full. "The tapestry that is modern eating is woven with influences from biology, psychology, and the food environment," writes Kelly D. Brownell, director of the Rudd Center for Food Policy and Obesity at the Yale Center for Eating and Weight Disorders.[1] He points out that biology can have an effect on such factors as the kind of food we choose, whether or not we feel satisfied after eating, and whether it is difficult or easy to lose weight. Yet our eating behaviors often are related to other aspects such as our social networks—our friends, classmates, relatives, and others with whom we associate on a regular basis.

These social relationships may have an impact on whether a person eats too much and gains weight. Many people say that when they hang out with friends they do what everyone else does. Suppose everyone in your group orders pizza; you may go along and do the same or share with others. If all your friends eat salads, perhaps you will make that choice. In other words, most of us are likely to be interacting with our companions rather than paying attention to what we are eating.

## Social Relationships

Researchers from Harvard Medical School and the University of California, San Diego, studied the data that had been collected over a period of thirty-two years on more than twelve thousand people. The scientists concluded that social ties "have a marked influence on weight gain." For example, if a person's close friend becomes obese, that person's chances of becoming obese increase 57 percent. The siblings of someone who becomes obese have a 40 percent increased risk of obesity, and the spouse of an obese person has a 37 percent increased risk.[2] The researchers published their findings in the July 26, 2007, edition of the *New England Journal of Medicine*. One of the principal investigators, Nicholas Christakis, a physician and professor of medical sociology at Harvard Medical School, pointed out:

Most likely, the interpersonal, social network effects we observe arise not because friends and siblings adopt each other's lifestyles. It's more subtle than that. What appears to be happening is that a person becoming obese most likely causes a change of norms about what counts as an appropriate body size. People come to think that it is okay to be bigger since those around them are bigger, and this sensibility spreads.[3]

The researchers stressed that their findings were not meant to encourage people to avoid fat friends or to blame someone else for their weight gain. But they did suggest that having a social network of thin people could influence one's eating behavior.

Kelly Brownell disagrees with the Harvard investigators' conclusions. He told a *New York Times* reporter, "I think there's a great risk here in blaming obese people . . . for things that are caused by a terrible environment."[4] In his book *Food Fight,* Brownell describes that environment as "toxic," that is, conditions in the United States and other industrialized countries are conducive to overeating, gaining weight, and putting people at risk for numerous health problems.

One part of that toxic environment is the supersize trend—fast-food meals, sandwiches, fries, superlarge soft drinks (such as the Big Gulp), and other items that have increased in size over the past few decades. Another is the widespread publicity given food-eating contests that exploit overeating by contestants who stuff themselves with hot dogs or gorge on pies or other foods just to see who can consume the most. One more factor is the availability of food (often junk food) around the clock in a variety of places, such as twenty-four-hour groceries, gas stations, interstate cafes, drugstores, and even hospital waiting rooms. Brownell's toxic environment also includes the popularity of TV shows, video games, computer chat rooms, and other sedentary activities that discourage regular exercise.

## Emotional Eating

In some cases, emotions trigger eating. Have you ever felt sad, lonely, bored, frustrated, or anxious and found yourself eating a candy bar, a bag of chips, fries, or a dish of ice cream to lift your spirits? A variety of foods can provide solace or comfort, and the choices depend on the individual. Many comfort foods are associated with a dish that a parent or caregiver prepared for you during early childhood. Maybe the comfort food is cookies with milk, bread pudding, macaroni and cheese, mashed potatoes, or some other simple dish.

Whatever the food, it may in some way brighten your mood. Thus eating becomes a quick antidote, a way to deal with negative emotions. Problems arise when comfort foods are high in calories and low in nutritional value. A person may be at risk for weight gain and unhealthy eating patterns, especially if eating becomes a habitual way of dealing with emotions.

Emotional eating is also prompted when people want to reward themselves for a job well done, a goal reached, or just because they think they deserve a treat. Maybe you want to celebrate an accomplishment, so you buy food and call your friends to "gather 'round the good stuff" (once a slogan for a Pizza Hut commercial). Consuming food may also be a way to calm excitement or intense joy.

Health experts and dietitians recommend that people learn what emotions or circumstances trigger eating. Then instead of going for food immediately, a person should choose an alternative—go for a walk, listen to music, call a friend, or take part in an activity that has nothing to do with food.

## Eating Habits

While our social networks and environment may contribute to unhealthy eating, personal habits also play a role and sometimes are entwined with environmental factors. Suppose someone always has a sweet snack after school or in the evening before bedtime. That could mean she or he has established an eating habit, one that may not be healthy. The same could be true if someone always has a high-calorie portion of popcorn when at the movies or watching TV at home.

Unhealthy eating may also be part of a person's daily lifestyle. A teenager on *Youth Radio Atlanta* put it this way:

> I tell myself every day that I am going to eat healthy. But just the other morning, I ate a bag of potato chips for breakfast. That was a bad decision. There were many other healthier foods in my house but the chips were the easiest to eat and I was being lazy.

**One difficulty in trying to eat healthfully is the constant availability of junk food from a variety of places.**

I'm a little frightened about the effects of my diet later in life. The more garbage I eat, the more unhealthy my body becomes. And as I get older, I remind myself to eat salads, fresh fruits and vegetables.

Kids of my generation are eating so much junk food, it's going to be hard to convince everyone to change. I saw my friend pile on the pounds from eating lots of fast food and now I'm worried about her.

I don't want to be one of those people who becomes heavy and then stays that way for the rest of their lives.[5]

Another eating habit that can be a health risk is always having a breakfast such as a cold cereal that is primarily sugar. (Some cereals contain more grams of sugar per serving than a chocolate bar.) One more unhealthy habit is to sprinkle lots of sugar on unsweetened cereal. Eating breakfast tarts each morning is another example. The label on a box of raspberry Pop-Tarts shows that they contain several forms of sugar, such as dextrose and high fructose corn syrup, in the raspberry filling as well as in the pastry itself. Donuts, sweet breads, pancakes and syrup, and white bread toast with jam or jelly are other examples of sugary breakfast items.

> **Sometimes we eat to relieve stress or to calm emotions. Other times we eat simply because people around us are doing so.**

Breakfast with high sugar and low fiber content might cause people to overeat. After eating, blood sugar levels go up and then drop quickly so that a person craves more food later on. Ultimately this leads to weight gain.

The customary breakfast for Brittany, a young Utah teenager on the verge of being obese, was a Toaster Strudel with squeezable icing and Lucky Charms, a brand of cold cereal consisting of frosted oats and colored marshmallows. But in seventh grade she became aware that her breakfast was making her feel ill. "It happened after first period," Brittany told a reporter. "First, I couldn't see right and then I'd get a huge migraine headache and throw up at school." As a result of feeling sick, Brittany would go home, miss classes, and have to make up the work. Her other eating habits were just as destructive. "I used to eat whatever I wanted," she said. "I would stuff myself until I was about to blow up."[6] She has changed to a healthy eating lifestyle, choosing salads, chicken, and fruit at the school cafeteria, eating small portions, and getting more exercise. And she is losing weight.

Skipping breakfast on a daily basis is another unhealthy habit, numerous studies have shown. "People who eat breakfast are significantly less likely to be obese and diabetic than those who usually don't," the American Heart Association reported in 2003. Researcher Mark A. Pereira noted: "It appears that breakfast may play an important role in reducing the risk of type 2 diabetes and cardiovascular disease."[7]

Many people omit breakfast as a means of losing weight, but that tactic does not really work. Those who do not eat breakfast tend to get overly hungry later in the day and start consuming snacks or overeating at lunch or dinner. Avoiding breakfast also makes it difficult to get the vitamins and other nutrients the body needs daily.

## Other Factors Contributing to Unhealthy Eating

Biology and family history can contribute to poor eating habits. Some studies have shown that even before a child is born, she or he may be "programmed" to prefer the taste of junk food if that is the mother's typical diet. Young people who grow up in a family whose diet consists primarily of starches and few fruits and vegetables are likely to follow the same pattern.

Poverty may also play a major role, although low income does not necessarily indicate that members of a family will have unhealthy diets or tend to be overweight. In recent years some studies have shown a link between poverty and obesity, while others have shown that poverty has little or no impact on obesity. If low-income family members are obese, one of the reasons could be that the foods the family can afford usually are those that are filling but high in calories. The U.S. Food Stamp Program, which in 2007 provided $1.05 per meal per person in food aid each month, helps those in poverty buy needed food.[8] But as the cost of food has been rising, it has become increasingly difficult to stretch food dollars to buy nutritious, low-calorie foods like fresh fruits and vegetables, fish, and lean meat. In addition, poor families may have limited access to nutritious foods, especially in inner-city neighborhoods where there are few if any supermarkets or fresh-food stands.

Low-income urban families may also have to use public transportation to get to a major grocery store, and returning on a bus or subway with bags of groceries can be difficult. The alternative may be to shop at a neighborhood store that sells lots of junk foods or to eat at a fast-food restaurant that offers large portions for a low price.

Yet healthy eating is possible, even on an extremely limited budget. And advice on a healthy diet is available from numerous sources. But people may not take advantage of such resources if they do not understand how their eating habits may damage their health. Becoming aware of the effects of unhealthy eating is a first step toward changing to a nutritious dietary plan.

# Effects of Unhealthy Eating

4

Over the past decade, the harmful effects of unhealthy eating have been publicized widely in the media, at schools, on Web sites, and elsewhere. At the same time, promotion and advertising of junk food and food lacking in needed nutrients have helped encourage unhealthy eating habits among American young people, medical experts say.

Frequently, TV advertising and marketing to children and adolescents are blamed for unhealthy eating habits. Michael McGinnis, chair of the Institute of Medicine's Committee on Food Marketing to Children, noted: "Marketing to kids is a $10 billion industry; new food and beverage products for kids rose tenfold between 1994 and 2004. There is just no question that children's diets are affected quite directly by marketing, especially TV marketing."[1]

The nonprofit Kaiser Family Foundation (KFF), which focuses on the nation's major health care issues, supports this opinion in its fifty-nine-page study—the largest ever conducted of TV food advertising. KFF researchers looked at a total of 1,638 hours of TV programming aimed at children aged 2–7, "tweens" aged 8–12, and teenagers 13–17. They analyzed nearly nine thousand food and beverage ads, and discovered that the 2–7 age group sees an average of twelve TV food ads a day on TV. The number increased for children aged 8–12 to twenty-one TV food ads a day. Teenagers 13–17 years old see on average seventeen TV food ads daily. None of the food advertisements analyzed were for fruits or vegetables, and more than half the ads were for candy, snacks, or fast food.[2] Researchers pointed out:

> [The] study does not address the issue of whether food advertising to children on TV is going up or down, nor does it address the issue of whether such advertising influences what kids eat, or should be in any way restricted, either through voluntary industry efforts or through regulatory policy. What it does indicate, however, is that food marketing is a predominant part of the television advertising landscape for children, and that young people's exposure to such messages is substantial, while their exposure to countervailing health messages on TV is minimal.[3]

Because of the public concern about unhealthy eating patterns that can lead to overweight and obesity among young people, some companies are taking part in the Children's Food and Beverage Advertising Initiative. Companies such as Campbell Soup, Coca-Cola, General Mills, Hershey, Kellogg, Kraft Foods, Mars, McDonald's, and PepsiCo have agreed to promote healthier products.

## Prevalence of Obesity

In 2007, another research team issued a report describing their study of obesity prevalence in the United States. A team from the Johns Hopkins Bloomberg School of Public Health analyzed data, journal papers, and surveys of adolescent health and risk behaviors, and published their findings in the medical journal *Epidemiologic Reviews*. They reported that 75 percent of Americans would be obese by 2015 if current trends continue. Some of their key findings were the following:

- Women 20–34 years old have the fastest increase rate of obesity and overweight.

- 80 percent of African-American women aged forty or older are overweight; 50 percent are obese.

- Asians have a lower obesity prevalence when compared to other ethnic groups. However, Asians born in the United

States are four times more likely to be obese than their foreign-born counterparts.

- People in the Southeast are more likely to be obese than are people on the West Coast, in the Midwest, or in the Northeast.

- 16 percent of all children and adolescents are overweight, and 34 percent are at risk of becoming overweight.

- African-American and Mexican-American children and adolescents are more likely to be overweight or at risk of overweight than their white counterparts.[5]

All groups cited in the study showed a consistent increase "in obesity or overweight prevalence, but the increase varied by group, making this public health issue complex," noted May A. Beydoun, coauthor of the study. "More research needs to be completed to look into the underlying causes."

## Diabetes

About 21 million American adults and children have diabetes, and more than 224,000 die annually from the disease. It is a disease in which the body does not produce or properly use insulin, a hormone that converts glucose (sugar) and starch (like potatoes) into energy the body cells need to function.

There are two types of diabetes: Type 1 and Type 2. Type 1, once known as juvenile diabetes, is diagnosed in young people whose bodies do not produce insulin; they may need several insulin injections per day or an insulin pump to survive. Type 2 diabetes is the more common form. It develops gradually as a person's body fails to produce enough insulin or to use insulin efficiently. Type 2 diabetes used to be

A study found that children aged 8–12 see an average of 21 food ads per day—more than half of them for candy, snacks, or fast food.

primarily an adult disease, but it has been rising steadily over the past decade in all children, especially African-American, Hispanic, American Indian, and some Asian young people.[6] Symptoms of diabetes include frequent urination, excessive thirst, extreme hunger, unusual weight loss, increased fatigue, irritability, and blurry vision.

While being overweight contributes to diabetes, other factors play a role as well. Some people may be at risk for diabetes because the disease runs in their families. Although diabetes is not inherited, some people may be born with genes that make them prone to becoming diabetic. Studies currently are under way to determine whether or how genes may cause diabetes.

## Some Myths and Facts About Diabetes

Many people believe that diabetes is caused by eating too many sweets. But the American Diabetic Association (ADA) calls that a myth. Consuming sugary foods and beverages can lead to weight gain, which, as mentioned, can be a risk factor in developing diabetes. However, as the ADA states: "If eaten as part of a healthy meal plan, or combined with exercise, sweets and desserts can be eaten by people with diabetes. They are no more 'off limits' to people with diabetes, than they are to people without diabetes." Other myths that the ADA has debunked include these:

- Some people believe diabetes is contagious. Diabetes is *not* an infection that you can catch like the flu.

- The notion that people with diabetes should eat special diabetic foods is a myth. According to the ADA:

    A healthy meal plan for people with diabetes is the same as that for everyone—low in fat (especially saturated and trans fat), moderate in salt and sugar, with meals based on whole grain foods, vegetables and fruit. Diabetic and dietetic versions of sugar-containing foods offer no special benefit. They still raise blood glucose levels, are usually more expensive and can also have a laxative effect if they contain sugar alcohols.[7]

- Some people are convinced that starchy foods like potatoes and pasta are not good for diabetics. Yet as ADA puts it, "Whole grain breads, cereals, pasta, rice and starchy vegetables like potatoes, yams, peas and corn can be included" in a healthy meal plan. "The key is portions. For most people with diabetes, having 3–4 servings of carbohydrate-containing foods is about right."[8]

## Heart and Breathing Problems

Just as unhealthy eating can lead to obesity, so it also can lead to heart disease and breathing problems. Heart disease includes heart attacks, high blood pressure, strokes, and atherosclerosis, or hardening of the arteries. Atherosclerosis restricts the ability of blood vessels to carry oxygen and nutrients from a person's heart to the rest of her or his body. One risk factor for atherosclerosis is eating lots of saturated fat. Lack of exercise, smoking, and being overweight are other risk factors for developing atherosclerosis and other heart diseases.

Unhealthy eating also can lead to breathing problems, especially if a person is extremely obese, as cited by the Medical College of Wisconsin report. One study of the relationship between unhealthy eating and respiratory illnesses was conducted by the Harvard School of Public Health and was published in *Chest*, a journal of the American College of Chest Physicians, in July 2007.

In the study of more than two thousand twelfth-grade students in the United States and Canada, researchers found that teens whose diet lacks vitamins C and E, beta carotene (a chemical that converts to Vitamin A), and omega-3 fatty acids are prone to breathing problems such as coughing, wheezing,

Foods such as these, which contain complex carbohydrates, are part of a healthy diet, even for people with diabetes.

bronchitis, and asthma (a chronic condition in which airways are inflamed). Vitamins C and E may "protect the lung from stress" and "omega-3 tends to reduce inflammation," the study's lead author Jane Burns told *U.S. News & World Report*.[9] There is added risk for teenagers who smoke and also have insufficient nutrients in their diet. They are four times more likely than their peers to develop lung problems.

## Harmful Dental Effects

As almost anyone who has been to a dentist knows, tooth decay occurs when plaque, a film of bacteria, stays on the teeth. The bacteria are fed by foods and beverages that contain sugar and starch, and they produce acids that can harm tooth enamel. When the harmful acids remain on the teeth, decay may result. Many people attempt to prevent this problem by brushing their teeth as frequently as possible.

Some eating habits also can have a detrimental effect on one's teeth. People who nibble on sugary snacks and sip soft drinks throughout the day may increase their risk of dental decay. Some starchy foods such as sweet breads and muffins may also contain sugars, honey, molasses, or syrups that react with bacteria to produce acids. Even fresh or dried fruit with high sugar content (raisins, sweet cherries, berries, and oranges, for example) has the potential to cause cavities. Fruits that are firm and crunchy, such as apples and pears, are better choices for snacking because they are not as likely to cling to the surface of the teeth. Cough drops and mints can be culprits, too. They should be used sparingly because the sugar in them coats the teeth and acts just like candy to promote decay.

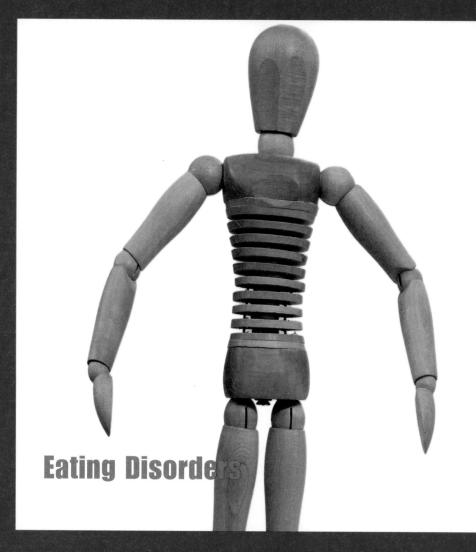

**5** **Eating Disorders**

An eating disorder (ED) is a psychological condition that includes a distorted view of self and extreme disturbances in eating behavior. One ED is anorexia nervosa, usually known simply as anorexia; another is bulimia nervosa, or bulimia.

The National Library of Medicine and the National Institutes of Health (NIH) define anorexia nervosa as

> an eating disorder in which a person refuses to stay at even the minimum body weight considered normal for [her or his] age and height. Persons with this disorder may have an intense fear of weight gain and a distorted body image. Inadequate eating or excessive exercising results in severe weight loss.[1]

In some cases, individuals may engage in both anorexic and bulimic behavior to control their weight.

The NIH also defines bulimia nervosa, sometimes called binge-purge behavior. This disorder "is an illness defined by food binges, or recurrent episodes of significant overeating, that are accompanied by a sense of loss of control." The NIH also notes, "The affected person then uses various methods—such as vomiting or laxative abuse—to prevent weight gain."[2]

While binge eating frequently occurs with bulimia, on its own it is another form of disordered eating. Sometimes it is called compulsive overeating. It may be a way to deal with stress, anxiety, or other negative emotions. Ron Saxen, a recovered binge eater, tells what it was like to gorge on food in his book *The Good Eater: The True Story of One Man's Struggle with Binge Eating Disorder*, published in 2007. Before overcoming his disorder, it was not unusual for him to consume "three Big Macs, a large order of fries, and a chocolate shake followed by four Hostess fruit pies, and a half gallon of Haagen-Dazs ice cream slathered with a pound of M&M's and a pint of hot fudge sauce."[3]

Usually, overeating creates guilt and even more stress and anxiety, so binge eaters repeat the practice, creating a cycle of overeating. Binge eaters are likely to be overweight or obese.

## Who Has Eating Disorders?

Studies conducted by government agencies, ED prevention organizations, and educational foundations measure the prevalence of eating disorders in the United States in different ways. Some assess ED prevalence only among females, while others collect data on both females and males in all segments of society. For example,

- The National Institute of Mental Health says that an estimated 0.5 to 3.7 percent of females in the United

States suffer or have suffered from anorexia nervosa in their lifetime.[4]

- The U.S. Substance Abuse and Mental Health Services Administration declares that 90 percent of people with eating disorders are women between the ages of 12 and 25.[5]

- Researchers at McLean Hospital (an affiliate of Harvard Medical School) collected information from more than nine thousand people across the United States. Among the results: 0.9 percent of women and 0.3 percent of men reported having anorexia nervosa at some point in their lives, and 1.5 percent of women and 0.5 percent of men reported having bulimia nervosa. Percentages were higher for binge eating disorder. The study found that 3.5 percent of women and 2 percent of men had it at some point in their lives.[6]

- The National Association of Anorexia Nervosa and Associated Disorders (ANAD) says that there are 7 million women and one million men in the United States with ED. Anorexic and bulimic individuals can be found in "all segments of society—the young and old, the rich and poor, and all ethnic groups including African American, Latino, Asian and Native American," according to ANAD.

## Causes of Anorexia and Bulimia

No one knows the exact causes of anorexia or bulimia, but one underlying factor is dissatisfaction with one's body image. Females want to be thinner and males want to be more muscular than they actually are. Both genders are influenced by society's and the media's portrayals of what is supposed to be an ideal body.

**ED and the Law**

In 2007, ANAD appeared before a congressional committee considering new legislation, the Mental Health and Addiction Equity Act. The legislation, if enacted, would remove major insurance restrictions and limitations on early access to treatment for eating disorders, which "cause tremendous suffering for victims and families," ANAD noted. "Eating disorders are treatable and sufferers can recover provided that they receive adequate treatment."[7]

Girls and women frequently are obsessed with losing weight, wanting to look like fashion models or female celebrities with extremely thin figures. Advertising for clothes, cosmetics, and other beauty products feature images of picture-perfect models that girls and young women admire. They also want to be attractive to boys and men who believe that the ideal female body is like that portrayed in fashion advertisements. Females with EDs hope to achieve a skinny version of beauty, even if it means being anorexic or bulimic.

Boys and men are also influenced by media images. They may resort to disordered eating to obtain the so-called ideal body type shown in advertisements for male cosmetics, hair and skin care, clothing, and other products. Males who are runners, dancers, jockeys, models, actors, entertainers, or in other professions requiring thinness frequently are at risk for EDs.

A need to be in control is another major characteristic of people with disordered eating behavior. In order to feel in charge, they refuse to eat, or they purge themselves of food. They may express pride in having the willpower to resist food, and if they are tempted to eat something they like, they feel guilty. In

**No one knows the exact causes of anorexia or bulimia, but one underlying factor is dissatisfaction with one's body image.**

some cases, a person with an ED may taste or chew food but spit it out before swallowing it.

EDs are coping skills, some experts say. Some people with eating disorders have been physically or sexually abused in their lives. They starve themselves into numbness so that they will not have to feel the effects of disappointing and damaging relationships.

Another aspect of eating disorders is perfectionism. People with EDs may try to achieve nearly impossible goals. In school they try to get perfect grades, seek perfect relationships, and attempt to develop perfect bodies. Thus, in their view, they gain a sense of power. However, the feeling of power is an illusion. "Inside they feel weak, powerless, victimized, defeated, and

**Both boys and girls are influenced by society's pressures to have a perfect body—pressure that may contribute to eating disorders.**

resentful," according to the organization Anorexia Nervosa and Related Eating Disorders, Inc. (ANRED). On its Web site, ANRED points out:

> People with eating disorders often lack a sense of identity. They try to define themselves by manufacturing a socially approved and admired exterior . . . by symbolically saying "I am, or I am trying to be, thin. Therefore, I matter."
>
> People with eating disorders often are legitimately angry, but because they seek approval and fear criticism, they do not dare express that anger directly. They do not know how to express it in healthy ways. They turn it against themselves by starving or stuffing.[8]

Some of the theories that have been proposed regarding the causes of eating disorders include genetic factors. Studies published in the *New England Journal of Medicine* in March 2003 indicated that for some people heredity plays a role in binge eating and the development of obesity. Brain chemistry may be a factor also. Imbalances in neurotransmitters, nerve cells that send messages from one cell to another, may be responsible for anorexic behavior in some people.

## Symptoms of Eating Disorders

While symptoms vary with individuals, people who have anorexia may diet, fast, or exercise excessively to lose pounds, in spite of the fact that they already are at an abnormally low weight. If they do eat, they are likely to consume only a few foods in small amounts. They may weigh their food and count calories. In an article for *Girls' Life*, teenager Jennifer Shiroky described some of the classic symptoms she exhibited with her ED behavior:

> At 13, I gained a little weight and became very self-conscious about my body. Suddenly, I was hyper-aware of what I put into my mouth and was dieting for the first time in my life. . . . Around that time, I radically changed my eating habits. I only allowed myself to

## Danger!—"Diabulimia"

Another form of purging that is extremely dangerous is "diabulimia." The term comes from Type 1 diabetics, primarily teenage girls, who try to lose weight by not taking their needed insulin. Some diabetics with this disorder reason that insulin causes weight gain so they can stay thin with smaller doses. Less insulin causes blood sugar to rise, and then a diabetic becomes very thirsty, drinking lots of water, urinating frequently, and getting rid of the sugar and extra weight in the urine.

If blood sugar is not maintained in a healthy manner, a diabetic is at great risk for damage to the eyes, nerves, and kidneys. Blindness and heart failure can result. An immediate danger is a diabetic coma requiring an emergency visit to the hospital.

eat a few specific foods, like cottage cheese and oatmeal, which I felt were "safe" since they wouldn't cause weight gain. I always skipped breakfast, but I ate "lunch" with friends in the cafeteria. My friends, who ate regular packed sandwiches and hot meals, sometimes asked why I was only eating a cereal bar. I always had an excuse, that I had wolfed a big breakfast or had eaten my lunch earlier. Since I always wore baggy clothes, no one really noticed how much weight I was losing.

Jennifer went on to explain that she became "so controlling about food" that she cooked the family meals, serving large portions to everyone except herself. She refused to take more food, and even became "mean" and "edgy," as she put it. "Inside, I was miserable and confused. Controlling my food intake had become a complete priority in my life."[9]

Like people with anorexia, those who have bulimia are obsessed with their weight. They may eat a large amount of food for a single meal and then immediately force themselves to vomit or use laxatives to get rid of what they consumed. This binge-purge cycle takes place on average fourteen times each week, experts say.

Warning signs that someone may have anorexia include dramatic weight loss over a short period of time, low body temperature (feeling cold much of the time), dry hair or skin, growth of baby-fine hair called lanugo on the body, swollen ankles and feet, fatigue, and in girls and women, cessation of menstrual periods. Signs of bulimia include erosion of tooth enamel (from frequent vomiting), frequent trips to the bathroom, and use of laxatives or syrup of ipecac (which causes vomiting). People with eating disorders tend to exhibit some antisocial behaviors such as avoiding events where food is served, refusing to eat with others or pretending to eat and throwing food away, and wearing oversized clothes to hide a thin body.

The binge-eating disorder is unlike bulimia in that people do not purge the food they eat. Symptoms may not be noticeable except for weight gain because binge eaters usually eat alone and may consume large amounts of food even though they do not feel hungry. Binge eating episodes are likely to occur several times per week.

## Effects of Eating Disorders

There is no question that EDs can cause serious damage to a person's health and may be life threatening. One complication of anorexia is electrolyte imbalance. Electrolytes are essential for many body functions. They exist in the blood and include salts and minerals such as sodium, calcium, potassium, chlorine, magnesium, and bicarbonate. Low levels of electrolytes can affect the body in many ways. Calcium deficiency, for example, can lead to low bone mass density. This in turn can lead osteoporosis, a condition in which the bones become porous, often resulting in bone fractures. Lack of potassium may result in muscle weakness, irritability, drowsiness, mental confusion, and irregular heartbeat.

Anorexia can also damage the heart, liver, and kidneys.

Starvation slows down body functions and causes low blood pressure, pulse, and breathing rate. As a result, an anorexic person may be light-headed and unable to concentrate. Depression is also common among anorexics, which sometimes leads to suicide. The risk of heart problems is ever present, which can be life threatening. In short, anorexia can kill.

Some researchers say that between 5 and 20 percent of those with anorexia die from the disorder. As ANRED puts it: "Without treatment, up to twenty percent (20%) of people with serious eating disorders die. With treatment, that number falls to two to three percent (2–3%)."[10] The death rate for anorexia nervosa is the highest of any mental illness.[11]

The damaging effects of bulimia include stomach pain and tooth decay from acids in the mouth due to vomiting. Because people with bulimia throw up frequently, their salivary glands may expand, creating "chipmunk cheeks." Purging through vomiting or laxative use can also cause potassium loss and dehydration.

People with EDs may resort to excessive exercise to lose weight. While exercise is important for good health, compulsive exercise could be a sign of an ED. Some may spend hours each day lifting weights, doing sit-ups, riding stationary bikes, using treadmills and other exercise equipment. Or they may run miles every day and wear heavy sweats over plastic wraps to increase perspiration and lose water weight. Excessive exercise can cause bone fractures and muscle strains.

Binge eating, as the Harvard study demonstrated, affects more people than anorexia or bulimia. The consequences to health "can be serious—including obesity, diabetes, heart disease, high blood pressure and stroke. It is imperative that health experts take notice of these findings," says the study's lead author, James I. Hudson, director of the Psychiatric Epidemiology Research Program at McLean Hospital and professor of psychiatry at Harvard Medical School.[12]

While health experts continue to warn about disordered eating, they also consistently urge people with EDs to find help. Numerous organizations are available for that purpose. ANRED is one; another is ANAD. Others include the National Eating Disorders Association, American Anorexia/Bulimia Association, Harvard Eating Disorders Center, and many local ED clinics, camps, and support groups. People who recover from disordered eating learn how to cope with their psychological condition and to eat in healthy ways.

Healthy Eating

For years, food guides in the United States have been provided by government agencies to educate people about healthy food choices. Dietitians, nutritionists, and medical experts also offer advice on healthy eating. So do the media. In other words, there is an abundance of information, and most of it is based on the *Dietary Guidelines for Americans* produced by the U.S. Department of Health and Human Services (DHHS) and the U.S. Department of Agriculture (USDA). In addition, the Food Pyramid created by the USDA frequently is used as a basis for how to eat in a healthful manner.

The purpose of the Dietary Guidelines is to "encourage

most Americans to eat fewer calories, be more active, and make wiser food choices," the publication states. The guidelines advise that foods are the best sources of nutrients and other compounds needed for good health. While vitamin and mineral supplements may be helpful, they "cannot replace a healthful diet."[1]

The current version of the USDA Food Pyramid below—MyPyramid—shows the various food groups recommended and their proportional amounts. Orange stands for whole grains, green for vegetables, red for fruits, yellow for oils, blue for dairy products, and purple for meat and beans. The figure climbing the stairs symbolizes the need for physical activity.

It appears on a Web site that allows you to interact and "go inside the pyramid" to "make smart choices from every food group."[2] You enter your age, height, weight, gender, and amount of physical activity to obtain your personal eating plan.

MyPyramid
STEPS TO A HEALTHIER YOU
MyPyramid.gov

GRAINS    VEGETABLES    FRUITS    MILK    MEAT & BEANS

What if you do not have a computer to access the Internet and calculate the amount of each food group that should be in your daily diet? You can order the Dietary Guidelines and the booklet *Finding Your Way to a Healthier You* from the U.S. Government Printing Office.

The Harvard School of Public Health has developed its own Healthy Eating Pyramid. It appears on the school's Web site, and it is published in *Eat, Drink, and Be Healthy* by Walter C. Willett, M.D. The book contradicts some of the USDA recommendations. It offers advice based on long-term studies well known throughout the world, such as the Health Professionals Follow-up Study, the Framingham Nurses' Health Study, and the Physicians' Health Study. The first study tracked thousands of individuals for more than twenty years. Numerous tables and charts in the book show, for example, the amounts of nutrients in foods. Others indicate the types of dietary fat and their effect on cholesterol, how nutrients are reduced when whole wheat flour becomes refined white flour, and what sources of protein are available other than meats. A final chapter offers healthful menus and recipes.

## Efforts to Put Healthy Foods in Schools

Because of concerns about the harmful health effects of junk food, schools across the United States have been replacing candy, chips, and sugary soft drinks with nutritious food and beverage items in vending machines. Similar changes have been taking place in school cafeterias.

To decrease overall consumption of junk foods among students, the Child Nutrition Promotion and School Lunch Protection Act (CNPSLP) was introduced in the U.S. Senate in 2006. It was reintroduced in the U.S. House in 2007. The bill would update the Child Nutrition Act of 1966, which applies to school cafeteria meals provided by federally funded food service programs. The 1966 act requires that school meals meet science-based nutritional standards established by Congress and the Secretary of Agriculture; however, food sold elsewhere on school campuses, such as in vending machines, school canteens, and snack bars, is not required to meet comparable nutritional standards. The proposed CNPSLP, however, would apply to all foods sold outside the school meal programs on a school campus at any time during the school day.

The legislative proposal is endorsed by such groups as the American Cancer Society, the National PTA, the American Dietetic Association, and the National Education Association, according to the *Washington Post*. In addition, the *Post* reported in April 2007 that "a prestigious scientific panel" of the Institute of Medicine "urged the government . . . to ban soft drinks, sugary snacks and other junk food from schools, saying the typical fare available in vending machines, at snack bars and at class birthday parties is contributing to the growing obesity of America's children." The panel also recommended discontinuing snacks such as candy bars and chips sold at fund-raisers held at schools and instead "should sell healthier options such as apples, carrot sticks, raisins, low-sugar cereals, whole-grain tortilla chips, granola bars and nonfat yogurt with no more than 30 grams of added sugar."[3]

Most states now mandate that their school vending machines offer healthy alternatives to such snacks as candy bars, sugary sodas, and fried chips. Water, sports drinks, juice, granola bars, and baked chips are some items offered instead.

School cafeterias also help students make healthful food choices. One example is Pinellas County, Florida, public schools in the Tampa Bay area. Cafeterias removed french fries from elementary school menus as a first step in 2000, and offers fries only twice per week in middle school. By the 2009–2010 school year, no fries will be served in elementary or middle schools. High school students can purchase only one order of fries at a time, and portions are limited to 4.5 ounces.

Additional steps to improve meals include low-fat vegetable side dishes, salads, vegetarian chili, and bean and cheese burritos.[4]

The New Jersey Agricultural Department requires the state's schools to reduce sugar, trans fat, and saturated fats in the foods they serve. In addition, foods and beverages listing sugar as their first ingredient and foods of low nutritional value are banned from school grounds. At first, high school senior Dennisha Scott was sure she would hate the new menu that included vegetable sandwiches, baked chips, and juice. But she and some of her classmates soon changed their opinions. As Scott told a reporter: "Eating healthy promotes healthy bodies. And healthy bodies mean healthy brains so you have a better thinking process, and you can concentrate on your schoolwork."[5] Out of 573 New Jersey school districts, more than 300 had adopted the new menus in early 2007.

**Most states now mandate that their school vending machines offer healthy alternatives to such snacks as candy bars, sugary sodas, and fried chips.**

Some colleges report that over the past few years there has been an increase in the number of students requesting and buying healthy foods. Food service directors are adding low-calorie, low-fat, and low-carbohydrate items as well as vegetarian options for students. Food stations with salads and fruits are also available. At the University of California Irvine, a Healthy Heart station features a complete meal that is less than 500 calories, contains no trans fat, and is low in salt, low in cholesterol, and sugar free.

Along with serving healthy meals, some universities have promoted ways to help students incorporate green vegetables into their diets. Students, for example, may learn how to eat green foods such as spinach omelets at breakfast. A promotional effort at Johns Hopkins University in Maryland highlighted vegetarian cooking with a dining services chef demonstrating

**Many schools are instituting healthier lunches in an effort to stem childhood obesity and build better eating habits.**

how to prepare a healthful vegetarian meal in a simple and efficient way.

Dining Services at the University of Connecticut supports and promotes a Local Routes program whose goal is to use local foods in its food service operations. A student-run EcoGarden near campus works with Local Routes to supply produce for the university's Whitney Dining Hall, where vegetarian and vegan meals are served. Local farms provide other foods, and in the dining hall, labels identify who provided the ingredients for various entrées. For example, nearby Franklin Mushroom Farm produces the main ingredients for Portobello mushroom burgers that are served. Cage-free eggs and mountain dairy milk are other items from local sources.[6]

## Grocery Store Shopping

Grocery stores are attempting to do their part to encourage healthy eating. Numerous stores provide information about the nutrient content of fresh vegetables and fruits either on charts or on produce shelves or bins. Fresh produce, whole grain breads, meats, seafood, and dairy products are on the perimeter of most large stores. So if a shopper wants to fill a cart with fresh food, the place to start is on the outer edges of the store.

When shopping for canned, frozen, or other packaged foods, the source for nutrient content is the information panel called the Nutrition Facts label, which, as described previously, shows the serving size, and how many calories per serving. The label also indicates the total amount of fat with a breakdown of saturated, polyunsaturated, monounsaturated, and trans fat; cholesterol; certain vitamins and minerals by percentage of daily value (%DV)—the recommended daily allowance for a nutrient based on a 2,000-calorie diet—sodium (salt), protein, sugar, and fiber content.

Ingredients on the label are listed beginning with the greatest amount to the least. Consider sugar and other forms of sugar, which include dextrose, fructose, high fructose corn syrup, fruit juice concentrates, honey, and molasses. If these sweeteners are high on the list, as they often are on the labels for cold cereal, pastries, and other processed foods, you may want to find a less sugary product and one that may be lower in calories and higher in nutrients.

The packaging on some food items may declare that a product has "50 percent less fat" or "half the salt." These can be meaningless terms unless a person knows what the product is being compared with—is it 50 percent of the same type and quantity of product? For example, a package of turkey bacon says that it has 65 percent less fat than pork bacon, so to truly compare, a person would have to know the amount of fat in both kinds of bacon. A label on a store brand of canned corn says "50 percent less salt," but it does not make a comparison with anything. However, the label likely means that can of corn has half the salt of the store's regular brand of canned corn. A quick check of the Nutrition Facts on both the regular and low-salt store brand of canned corn shows the regular canned corn contains 310 milligrams of sodium (salt) and the other contains 150 milligrams of sodium—50 percent less salt than the regular canned corn.

Health and nutrition assertions are a different story. The federal Nutrition Labeling and Education Act requires that certain food claims abide by explicit rules. If the term "free" is used, the product must contain no amount, or only trivial amounts, of a specific ingredient. The terms "sugar free" and "fat free," for example, mean less than 0.5 grams of sugar or fat per serving. If a "low fat" claim is made, the product must have no more than 3 grams of fat per serving. "Low sodium" means less than 140 milligrams of salt per serving, "very low sodium" is 35 milligrams or less per serving, while "sodium free" means less than 0.5 milligrams of salt. One serving of a "low calorie" product must contain no more than 40 calories.

To help grocery shoppers choose healthy foods, the AHA created a heart-check symbol certifying that the product with the red heart and white check mark is low in saturated fat and cholesterol. (The AHA cautions that its certification program is designed for healthy people and that anyone with a medical condition should see a physician or dietitian before making changes to her or his diet.)

Anyone with access to the Internet can create a personalized heart-healthy grocery list online from more than eight hundred foods listed as low in saturated fat and cholesterol on the AHA Web site. Choices can be made by food type or manufacturer. Once products are selected, a list can be printed to take along to the store.[7]

## Shopping on a Budget

For families with limited income, it is not easy to buy healthy food. Millions of low-income families use food stamps (funded by the federal government). The stamps will buy between twenty-one dollars and twenty-five dollars worth of groceries each week. That translates to around $3.00 per day or $1.00 to $1.19 per meal.

In June 2007, four members of the U.S. Congress called attention to the difficulty of eating healthy meals with food stamps. They took the Congressional Food Stamp Challenge and spent only three dollars for food each day. Representative Barbara Lee of Oakland, California, took part and reported that one day she "had grits and toast for breakfast, crackers and a banana for lunch and two hamburgers from White Castle ($.51 apiece) for dinner." Another day she found a discount grocery store to buy "a small container of chicken and dumplings, an apple, a can of tuna, a box of macaroni and cheese and a can of turnip greens (total $2.25)." By the middle of the week, she reported: "It's hard to concentrate for any length of time on anything except food. I don't know how people with no money for decent meals do anything—study, work, exercise, read, have fun, etc. It's all about just making it through the day."[8]

In spite of the problems of eating healthfully on a tight budget, Congresswoman Jo Ann Emerson of Missouri, who also participated in the challenge, said planning carefully was an important element. As nutritionists and dietitians advise, a plan for grocery shopping should focus on creating meals around vegetables, grains, and fruit, not meat and prepared items. Other money-saving suggestions include stocking up on staples such as beans, brown rice, pasta, oatmeal, and barley. These can stretch soups, stews, and casseroles and add fiber. Using store coupons saves on grocery bills, as does shopping for produce in season and for sale items in the canned and frozen-food sections.

## Food Advertising

Whether or not cost is a factor in grocery shopping, healthy eating means being aware of how TV advertising affects food choices, especially if children go along to the grocery store. Youngsters frequently beg for products such as sugary cereals and high-calorie snacks endorsed by their favorite cartoon characters.

Nevertheless, some changes are taking place. Disney, Cartoon Network, and Discovery Communications are just

**Part of healthy eating is careful shopping. Reading labels can teach the consumer about a food's nutrient content.**

three of the companies that announced in 2007 that they are prohibiting the use of their company-owned characters to promote foods and beverages high in fat, calories, and sugar. Instead, advertised items must meet specific limits for these ingredients.

Food and beverage companies are also getting on board with changes in their advertising directed at children. Cadbury Adams, Campbell Soup, Coca-Cola, General Mills, Hershey, Kellogg, Kraft Foods, Mars, McDonald's, PepsiCo, and Unilever are taking part in the Children's Food and Beverage Advertising Initiative. These companies have agreed to promote healthier products. The Council of Better Business Bureaus will monitor whether companies are complying with the initiative's guidelines.

Critics say there are major loopholes in the marketing plan. Michael F. Jacobson, executive director for the Center for Science in the Public Interest (CSPI), called the guidelines for ads "pathetic" and suggested that Ronald McDonald riding a bicycle while eating a Big Mac or large order of fries would be considered a healthy lifestyle message. CSPI has issued its *Guidelines for Responsible Marketing for Children*, which can be accessed on the Internet.[9]

Another critic is Senator Tom Harkin of Iowa, who has long argued that food marketers should change how they advertise to children. According to his view, the initiative "leaves companies significant leeway to continue marketing unhealthy foods to kids. And ultimately, the new initiative is only as good as the enforcement."[10]

Currently, it is debatable whether the marketing strategy to limit junk food ads aimed at children will be successful. The fact remains that hundreds of TV commercials for foods and beverages with little nutrient value are aired daily and can influence viewers, no matter what their age group.

# Weight-Loss Diets and Pills

Healthy eating certainly involves a daily plan that provides adequate nutrients and helps a person maintain an appropriate weight. But many people who try to achieve the "perfect" weight turn to quick weight-loss diets and diet pills and supplements (vitamins, minerals, and herbs), which can be expensive, ineffective, and even dangerous.

Teenagers, especially females, are likely to try the latest diet advertised, and risk engaging in disordered eating behaviors, according to a study of more than twenty-five hundred junior high and high school students. In "Project EAT" (Eating Among Teenagers), the University of Minnesota's School of

Public Health surveyed teens in the 1998–1999 school year and followed up with another survey in 2003–2004. Girls in middle school who read dieting articles were twice as likely five years later to try to lose weight by fasting or smoking cigarettes, compared to girls who never read such articles, the study found. The researchers concluded:

> Frequent reading of magazine articles about dieting/weight-loss strongly predicted unhealthy weight-control behaviors in adolescent girls, but not boys. . . . Findings from this study, in conjunction with findings from previous studies, suggest a need for interventions aimed at reducing exposure to, and the importance placed on, media messages regarding dieting and weight loss.[1]

## What Are Weight-Loss Diets?

Anyone who has ever done a search on the Internet to find information about weight-loss diets knows that hundreds of thousands of "hits" appear. Millions of people look for a quick fix to their weight problems. Some dieters choose all-liquid diet plans that focus on drinking protein drinks, tea, apple cider vinegar, or other liquids while eliminating other foods. Or they might try diets that call for eating primarily a single food such as the Grapefruit Diet or the Cabbage Soup Diet. Grapefruit can help curb appetite before a meal or it can be a nutritious snack, but it has no special qualities to burn off fat. Cabbage soup can be a healthy meal, but eating it for most meals can cause bloating and gas. In short, neither all-liquid diets nor single-food diets are nutritionally sound. The American Heart Association puts it this way:

> Quick-weight-loss diets usually overemphasize one particular food or type of food. They violate the first principle of good nutrition: Eat a balanced diet that includes a variety of foods. If you are able to stay on a quick weight-loss diet for more than a few weeks, you may develop nutritional deficiencies, because no one type of food has all the nutrients you need for good health. . . . There are no

"superfoods." That's why you should eat moderate amounts from all food groups, not large amounts of a few special foods. These diets also violate a second important principle of good nutrition: Eating should be enjoyable. These diets are so monotonous and boring that it's almost impossible to stay on them for long periods.[2]

Popular weight-loss diets include low-carbohydrate (low-carb) and high-protein diets such as the Atkins Diet, South Beach Diet, and the Zone Diet. The Atkins Diet is one of the most widely used low-carb diets. The diet severely limits high-carb food—breads, pasta, fruits, sugar, and some vegetables. But the diet allows unlimited amounts of protein.

Ever since it was initiated in the 1970s, the Atkins Diet has been controversial. Some health experts consider the diet dangerous because it limits carbohydrates the body needs and allows protein foods high in saturated fats, which increases the risk of heart disease and obesity. People on the Atkins Diet may lose weight quickly in the short term because they lose water at first, but over the long time Atkins dieters lose no more weight than people on a low-fat, low-calorie diet, some researchers say.

Among the popular diets are detox diets that promise quick weight loss and disease prevention by supposedly cleansing the body of toxins or poisons. Hundreds of books and magazine articles tout these diet plans, which are based on the premise that we take in many toxic materials in foods and chemicals in the environment, and that we need to remove these poisons from our bodies. Certain foods and liquids are supposed to detoxify and not only reduce pounds but also offer benefits ranging from increased energy to reversal of cancer.

Detox diets frequently begin with fasting for a few days and then extremely limit foods or require a liquid diet of various concoctions, such as one made of lemon juice, maple syrup, water, and cayenne pepper. Laxatives may also be part of the regimen, which can last from a week to ten days.

Health experts warn against such diets. The Mayo Clinic, for example, says: "There is no evidence that detox diets actually remove toxins from the body. Most toxins in the body are very efficiently and effectively removed by the kidneys and liver and excreted in urine and stool."[3]

Teenagers especially need to be cautious about detox plans or any severe food restrictions or long fasts. Detox diets lack the nutrients that teens require for their growth and development. Athletes and teens involved in daily physical activities require enough food for energy; fasting and detox diets do not provide the needed calories.

Some diet programs do encourage a variety of healthy food choices. Two examples are Weight Watchers and the Jenny Craig Diet Program. There are few if any forbidden foods, but dieters are advised to limit calories. Both programs have support systems to help dieters establish and maintain a healthy eating pattern.

Whatever the weight-loss diets, they are usually widely advertised—on TV, the Internet, billboards, and in the print media. Their claims should be looked at critically. They may be suspect if they state that a dieter will lose more than one or two pounds per week; if they promise weight loss on a continual basis without exercising; if they limit food choices and do not offer a balanced diet that meets nutritional needs; if they say their product has been tested by a respected or leading medical center or university but provide no information on who, where, and how the study was conducted; or if they present testimonials from clients or "experts" who might be paid for their endorsements. To be safe, advice about a weight-loss diet should come from your family doctor, nurse, reputable nutritionist, dietitian, or health organization. In short, "the only sensible way to lose weight and maintain a healthy weight permanently is to eat less and balance your food intake with physical activity," as the AHA points out.[4]

## Myths About Dieting

The U.S. Department of Health and Human Services, other government agencies, and private health organizations have warned consumers about dieting myths, countering them with factual information. Some of these are below:

Myth: Quick weight-loss diets result in permanent weight loss.
Fact: It is possible to lose weight at first, but diets that limit food choices may result in lost nutrients the body needs.

Myth: High-protein/low-carbohydrate diets are a healthy way to lose weight.
Fact: The long-term health effects of such diets are unknown.

Myth: Starches are fattening and should be limited when trying to lose weight.
Fact: Many starchy foods are low in fat and calories and an important source of energy; if eaten in large portions and with toppings like butter and cheese they can become high in fat and calories.

Myth: Certain foods can help burn fat and lose weight.
Fact: No foods can burn fat.

Myth: "Natural" or herbal weight-loss products are safe and effective.
Fact: Such products usually are not scientifically tested for safety or effectiveness.

Myth: People can lose weight by eating whatever they want.
Fact: To lose weight, a person should limit the calories and portions of the foods.

Myth: People can lose weight by not eating.
Fact: Anyone who starves can lose pounds, but will also lose nutrients and muscle mass; pounds will return when a person starts eating again.

Myth: Fast foods are always an unhealthy choice for dieters.
Fact: Fast foods can be part of a diet plan if a person carefully selects small portions of low-calorie items.[5]

## Diet Pills

Diet pills and herbal supplements may also pose risks to people trying to lose weight. Among the risk takers are young teenagers. According to a University of Minnesota study, the proportion of high school-aged females who used diet pills nearly doubled—from 7.5 percent to 14.2 percent—over the five-year study period from 1999 to 2004. Twenty percent of the females surveyed had used diet pills by the age of twenty. "These numbers are startling, and they tell us we need to do a better job of helping our daughters feel better about themselves and avoid unhealthy weight control behaviors," noted Dianne Neumark-Sztainer, University of Minnesota professor and researcher.[6]

**Teenagers especially need to be cautious about detox plans or any severe food restrictions or long fasts.**

The Food and Drug Administration does not have the same rigorous standards for dietary supplements as it does for prescription drugs or medications sold over the counter (OTC). The FDA explains that it

> regulates dietary supplements under a different set of regulations than those covering "conventional" foods and drug products (prescription and Over-the-Counter). . . . The dietary supplement manufacturer is responsible for ensuring that [the] supplement is safe before it is marketed. FDA is responsible for taking action against any unsafe dietary supplement product after it reaches the market. Generally, manufacturers do not need to register their products with FDA nor get FDA approval before producing or selling dietary supplements.... Manufacturers must make sure that product label information is truthful and not misleading.[7]

Weight-loss aids may be labeled as supplements so that they "can be marketed with limited proof of effectiveness or safety," according to the Mayo Clinic. Vendors can make health claims about products based on their own review and interpretation of studies without the authorization of the FDA. Most of these

**A dieter calculates the caloric value of a meal. Some weight-loss programs help people learn to eat a more healthy diet, while others promise dramatic results with no effort.**

over-the-counter drugs "haven't been proved safe and effective, and some are downright dangerous," according to the Mayo Clinic.[8] Many decrease appetite but have no proven ability to reduce a person's weight, and may cause gastrointestinal or other problems.

Some products contain ephedra, also known as ma huang, a traditional Chinese medicine that acts like amphetamines or "uppers." Ephedra has been banned in the United States, but it is still sold on the Internet and is legally available in tea. Ephedra "can cause high blood pressure, heart rate irregularities, sleeplessness, seizures, heart attacks, strokes and even death," the Mayo Clinic health staff reports.[9]

Like advertising for weight-loss diets, claims about the effectiveness of diet pills and supplements can be misleading or fraudulent. In January 2007, the Federal Trade Commission (FTC) announced that the agency had fined marketers of OTC weight-loss and weight-control drugs Xenadrine EFX, TrimSpa, CortiSlim, and Bayer AG's One-A-Day WeightSmart a total of $25 million for false advertising. The ads included claims of rapid weight loss and reduction in osteoporosis and Alzheimer's disease. No scientific evidence supported the declarations. As part of the settlement with FTC, the companies were allowed to continue marketing the drugs but agreed to drop their false assertions. In a CNN report, FTC Chairman Deborah Platt Majoras warned: "You won't find weight loss in a bottle of pills that claims it has the latest scientific breakthrough or miracle ingredient. Paying for fad science is a good way to lose cash, not pounds."[10]

## Fast-Food Claims

Although many fast-food restaurants advertise or promote low-calorie items on their menus, that does not mean that a total meal will actually have a low caloric content. Customers frequently forget the calories in side dishes or soft drinks that they order. A feature in the fall 2007 issue of the *Journal of Consumer Research*, published by the University of Chicago, explains that people who frequent fast-food restaurants considered "healthy" (such as Subway) "over-generalize" such a claim. "In fact, consumers chose beverages, side dishes, and desserts containing up to 131 percent more calories when the main dish was positioned as 'healthy,'" researchers found. So the meal ends up containing more calories than the featured low-calorie main course.[11]

In attempts to provide fast-food patrons with more

comprehensive information about their calorie intake, some states, counties, and cities are considering legislation similar to New York City's calorie labeling rule. The regulation, which became effective in October 2007, requires fast-food and other chain restaurants to post calorie information for items on their menus. The city ordinance only affects restaurants that already present public information regarding nutrient content such as on a Web site or in a brochure.

The New York State Restaurant Association challenged the city ordinance, declaring it was too expensive to implement and would do little if anything to prevent people from eating foods high in calories. Other critics argue that it is not the responsibility of any government to see that people eat healthfully. In their view, this amounts to a "nanny state"—having someone constantly watching over the public and interfering with free choice.

Supporting the legislation are the organizations Public Citizen and the Center for Science in the Public Interest plus prominent health organizations, nutrition professors, and government officials. According to Public Citizen:

> American adults and children consume about one-third of their calories from restaurants and other food-service establishments, and studies link frequent eating out with obesity and higher caloric intakes. Without nutrition information, it is difficult for consumers to make informed choices. In requiring fast-food restaurants to disclose calorie information on their menus, New York City has taken the lead in addressing one of the largest contributors to the nation's obesity epidemic.[12]

## Portion Control

Even if you are able to check out the calories and nutrients in restaurant food, the information may not help much if you do not control the portions you eat. Whether we eat out or at home, most of us misjudge the amount of food or beverage we consume, which can easily result in taking in more calories than expected. Some restaurant menus and all packaged, canned, or bottled groceries show serving sizes, which vary depending on the item. But how do you determine a serving size when you are away from home and do not have any kind of measurement tool? The federal Weight-control Information Network (WIN) program suggests visualizing and comparing with everyday objects as a guide:

- 3 ounces of meat or poultry = a deck of cards

- 1 cup of cereal = a fist

- 1/2 cup of cooked rice, pasta, or potato = 1/2 baseball

- 1 baked potato = a fist

- 1 medium fruit = a baseball

- 1/2 cup of fresh fruit = 1/2 baseball

- 1 1/2 ounces of low-fat or fat-free cheese = 4 stacked dice

- 1/2 cup of ice cream = 1/2 baseball

- 2 tablespoons of peanut butter = a Ping-Pong ball

Another way to control portions when eating out is to order a small, children's-size meal, or before you start eating, ask for a take-home box to save half your meal. Eating a salad before lunch or dinner can help curb appetite and the temptation to eat a large meal. One more tip from WIN: Stop eating when you begin to feel full. Finally, no fad diet or pill is a substitute for nutritious foods in sensible portions to reach and stay at a healthy weight.[13]

## Choosing the Vegetarian Way

"Going vegetarian" is an option that an increasing number of teenagers and preteens are choosing. Although only a minority of teens make such a choice, parents, public health officials, school personnel, and others frequently ask: Is a vegetarian diet healthy? Answers come from many quarters. As might be expected, vegetarian groups highly endorse such a diet. Some medical groups do also, but with cautionary notes. The American Heart Association, for example, says:

> Many studies have shown that vegetarians seem to have a lower risk of obesity, coronary heart disease (which causes heart attack), high blood pressure, diabetes mellitus, and some forms of cancer.

Vegetarian diets can be healthful and nutritionally sound if they're carefully planned to include essential nutrients. However, a vegetarian diet can be unhealthy if it contains too many calories and not enough important nutrients.[1]

A research report in the *Journal of Pediatric Health Care* noted: "Many well-designed studies have concluded that children and adolescents who follow a properly designed vegetarian diet grow and develop normally." In addition, the report states:

> Research has highlighted nutritional advantages to vegetarian diets and has indicated that this style of eating can lead to lifelong healthy eating habits when adopted at a young age. Studies show that children and adolescents who follow a vegetarian diet have a lower intake of cholesterol, saturated fat, and total fat and a higher intake of fruit, vegetables, and fiber than their nonvegetarian counterparts.[2]

Dietitians also support the health aspects of a vegetarian diet. In a position statement published in the *Journal of the American Dietetic Association*, the ADA and Dietitians of Canada stated: "Appropriately planned vegetarian diets are healthful, nutritionally adequate, and provide health benefits in the prevention and treatment of certain diseases."[3]

## What Is a Vegetarian?

The term *vegetarian* can be confusing, because there are several types of vegetarians. Basically, a vegetarian does not eat meat, fish, or fowl, or products made with these foods; beyond this, there are a number of diverse eating patterns. For example, a vegan (usually pronounced VEE gun) eats only plant foods: fruits, vegetables, legumes (such as dried beans and peas), grains, seeds, nuts, and soy products. A lacto-vegetarian eats plant foods plus cheese and other dairy products. Lacto-ovo vegetarians do not eat meat, fish, or poultry, but along with plant foods, eat eggs, milk, and dairy products like cheese and yogurt. Some people consider themselves semi-vegetarians—

they do not eat red meat but include chicken and fish with plant foods, dairy products, and eggs.

Because a vegan diet does not include animal products, protein, vitamin B-12, vitamin D, iron, and calcium may be in short supply. But there are alternatives to animal products.

A vegetarian does not eat meat, fish, or fowl, or products made with these foods; beyond this, there are a number of diverse eating patterns.

Protein is found in soybeans, legumes, nuts, seeds, and whole grains. Enriched cereals and fortified soy contain B-12, needed by red blood cells. Iron is also an essential component of red blood cells and can be found in dark green vegetables (broccoli, romaine lettuce, and other leafy greens), dried beans and peas, lentils, and whole-grain products.

Lacto and lacto-ovo vegetarians obtain their protein and calcium from dairy products. Other major protein sources include beans, nuts, and soy products. For lacto-ovos, eggs are a protein source as well.

## Why Choose Vegetarianism?

Health concerns are not the only reason people choose to follow vegetarian diets. Being a vegetarian sometimes involves political, religious, or ethical views. For example, since about the 1960s, animal-rights groups have been politically active in spreading their message that nonhuman animals have a right to be free from pain and suffering and that slaughtering animals for food is cruel, unhealthy, and immoral. Morally inspired vegetarians are generally antiviolence, and some believe that there is no difference between meat eaters and cannibals—both eat meat derived from animals, they contend. In addition, such ethical vegetarians argue that the earth's productive land could grow much more food for humans per acre if grains, vegetables, and other plant foods were raised for human consumption rather than grains only for animal feed.

Among religious vegetarians are Seventh-Day Adventists, a Protestant group that advocates a vegetarian diet as part of its spiritual and health practices. Health emphasis has been part of the church since its beginning in the 1860s. One of its leaders, Mrs. Ellen G. White, believed that any abuse of the body was a violation of God's temple. Long before nutrition became a science, White was advising Adventists to eat a well-balanced diet; to eat natural foods in season; to avoid meat, especially animal fat; and to reject refined foods such as white sugar and flour, which she believed even then to be lacking in nutrients.

Today, the Seventh-Day Adventist church includes health and healing practices as a basic part of its teachings. The church operates hospitals, clinics, university medical schools and centers. Health food industries are part of the church complex also. Food companies affiliated with the Adventists process and package goods that contain no meat, animal shortening, or refined sugar or flour.

Several other religious groups in the United States practice vegetarianism. For instance, many Hindus (but not all) avoid meat, a practice based on veneration of the life cycle. Most do not eat beef. Thousands of years ago, Hindus in India placed a taboo on killing cows except in times of famine. Since then the cow has been considered sacred in Hinduism.

Other eastern religions also practice vegetarianism. Jains, followers of an ancient religion that developed along with Hinduism and Buddhism in India, believe that it is wrong to kill any living creature and practice *ahimsa*—a Sanskrit word for nonviolence. Buddhism and Taoism are two more religions that encourage vegetarian eating as a means of respecting nature and living beings.

In recent years, an increasing number of Christians of diverse denominations have chosen vegetarian lifestyles as a component of their religious beliefs. One group that espouses this view is the international Christian Vegetarian Association

### Some Common Vegetarian Food Items

Newcomers to vegetarian eating are certainly familiar with vegetables, fruits, and nuts, but they may not know about other items that are common in a vegetarian diet. They include:

brewer's yeast—A nutritional yeast not used for baking but a good source of B vitamins and protein that can be added to a variety of foods.

bulgur wheat—A whole grain that is parboiled, dried, then cracked. When soaked it becomes fluffy and can be used in many dishes.

hummus—A puree of chickpeas and sesame seed paste seasoned with lemon juice and garlic used as a spread and dip.

kefir—A cultured milk product that is like liquid yogurt.

millet—A grain that can be used in place of rice and provides protein.

miso—A fermented soybean paste that is a base for soups and a source of protein.

tempeh—A meat substitute made from soybeans.

tofu—A curd made from soybean milk that is curdled in much the same way as cow's milk is curdled for cottage cheese.

(CVA), which spreads its message on its Web site and at church conventions. One part of its mission is "To show the world that plant-based diets represent good, responsible Christian stewardship for all God's Creation." On its Web page, the CVA also states: "We encourage vegetarianism because the diet is ecologically sound, helps alleviate world hunger, and benefits human health."[4]

Recipes for vegetarian dishes are available on the Internet, in hundreds of books about vegetarianism, cookbooks, newspapers, and magazines. Some recipes are based on ethnic cuisine—flavors from Greece, Italy, Asia, and Latin America. Tabouli, for example, is a popular Mediterranean dish that many vegetarians enjoy. It is made with two cups of bulgur wheat soaked in one cup of warm or boiling water. The wheat is then mixed with chopped scallions, parsley, tomatoes, and a mixture of 1/4 cup lemon juice and 1/2 cup olive oil, garlic salt, and pepper to taste. The tabouli is usually placed in the refrigerator for a few hours to allow the flavors to blend.

Because hamburgers are such popular American fare, a vegetarian substitute can be made with tofu and potatoes. In a blender, grind two small peeled potatoes and 12 ounces of firm tofu with 1/4 cup each of garbanzo beans, whole wheat flour, and chopped walnuts, two small onions, one vegetable bullion cube, one tablespoon dry yeast, and salt, pepper, garlic powder, and soy sauce to taste. Make patties from the mixture and brown on both sides in a fry pan.

## Eating Vegetarian Meals

Is it difficult to make the transition from a meat-based diet to vegetarian eating? That is a question many people ask. The answer is simply "no" if a person starts with meals that he or she usually eats. For example, refried vegetarian beans can be substituted for the meat in a burrito (and if dairy products are used, add cheese). Chili can be made without meat by substituting textured vegetable protein. The other ingredients could include red beans or kidney beans, tomato sauce, onions, green pepper, and other vegetables of one's choice. Chili mac can consist of the chili ingredients plus macaroni and corn.

A pizza made with pita bread, tomato sauce, and vegetables is a good substitute for a meat-covered pizza whether made at home or ordered from a fast-food source. Tacos with refried vegetarian beans and vegetables, and vegetable stir-fry with tofu served with brown rice are two more simple alternatives. Other alternatives include a vegetable fajita, vegetable stews, and soups made with a vegetarian broth. There are also ready-made items

Vegetarian eating doesn't just mean salads. Here are some delicious alternatives (clockwise from top left): veggie burger, sushi, falafel, and couscous.

in supermarkets such as veggie burgers, veggie hot dogs, soy pepperoni, and cheese slices.

Salads, of course, are easily part of a vegetarian diet when they are made without meat or poultry toppings. Cheese and eggs may be eliminated also for some vegetarians. A favorite salad for many vegetarians is made with beans—kidney beans, garbanzo beans, green and wax beans, onions, and a sweetened vinegar dressing. Fruit salad is another popular option.

What about eating at the school cafeteria? In some cases, vegetarian students make and bring their lunches from home. Colleges are more likely to offer vegetarian foods in cafeterias and dorms than are secondary schools. But some middle schools and high schools do offer vegetarian items or have stations for vegetarian foods, such as salads and cheese pizza. The latter can be greasy and unpalatable and taboo for vegetarians who do not eat dairy products. However, a few schools are starting vegetarian lunch lines that offer much more variety, from pasta salad to veggie egg rolls.

Is it possible for a vegetarian to eat out? Many large cities now have vegetarian or "vegetarian friendly" restaurants, which are listed in the advertisement pages of telephone books or in tour guides. Vegetarian dishes are also available in fast-food restaurants ranging from Applebee's to Wendy's. Some menus explain whether meat fats are used in cooking and whether dairy products are contained in baked goods.

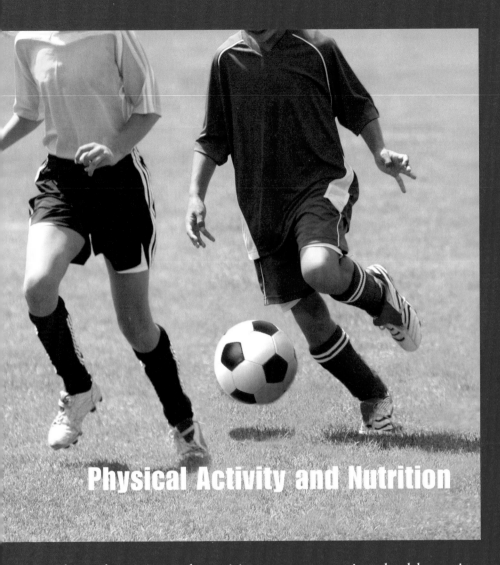

# Physical Activity and Nutrition

Physical activity and nutrition are partners in a healthy eating plan. That is clearly pictured on the USDA's MyPyramid and the Harvard Medical School Pyramid. "Fitness and good nutrition are hallmarks of successful learning and high achievement by students. They are critically important during the rapid mental and physical growth and development that occurs from birth through adolescence," says the National Education Association (NEA).[1]

Even as many Americans, including students from the elementary grades through high school, are learning about nutrition, they are not getting sufficient exercise. "As children exercise less, and drink less milk and more soda, they do not achieve peak bone mass in their early years. This increases their risk for bone fractures and osteoporosis later in life, particularly for girls," the NEA points out.[2]

The lack of regular physical activity and unhealthy eating "are responsible for at least 300,000 preventable deaths each year," says the National Conference of State Legislatures. "Regular physical activity provides short-term benefits, such as alleviating symptoms of anxiety and depression, and reduces long-term risks for disability and premature death."[3] Physical activity lowers the risk of numerous diseases, such as heart disease and obesity, helps control weight, and contributes to healthy bones, muscles, and joints.

## Physical Activity and Academic Performance

Researchers at the California Department of Education, Michigan State University, and others have studied students who have participated in vigorous physical activities like orga-nized sports and skateboarding. These students were more likely than nonactive students to achieve in such subjects as math, English, and science. The Michigan State study, which was pub-lished in the August 2006 *Medicine & Science in Sports & Exercise*, determined that P.E. classes that included on average nineteen minutes of moderate activity had no effect on student grades. But "higher grades were associated with vigorous physi-cal activity, particularly activity meeting recommended Healthy People 2010 levels."[4] Healthy People 2010 is managed by the CDC and establishes goals for good health for various age groups. For example, the Healthy People goal for adolescent exercise is to increase the proportion of adolescents who engage in moderate physical activity for at least thirty minutes five or more days per week. Another goal is to increase the proportion of adolescents who engage in vigorous physical activity that promotes heart and respiratory fitness three or more days per week for twenty or more minutes per occasion.[5]

Students who are involved in physical activities appear to function better academically than those who are not as active. There have not been enough studies to say conclusively whether there is a direct link between physical activity and brain function. But some physically active students do exhibit such benefits as high self-esteem and energy.

## Physical Education in Schools

Every five years, the National Association for Sport and Physical Education (NASPE) and the AHA produce a report titled *Shape of the Nation*. In the 2006 report, most states received an "F" in P.E. "This report shows that state physical education requirements are extremely weak," NASPE President Jacalyn Lund declared. "Furthermore, a vast array of 'loopholes' such as exemptions, waivers and on-line physical education classes too often eradicate those minimal standards at the local level at a time when more and more children are obese or at risk of obesity."[6]

Across the nation, states have dropped requirements for physical education (gym classes) in order to concentrate instead on academic subjects. Because of the federal No Child Left Behind Act, passed in 2001, schools must test students for academic performance. Physical education is not part of the testing, nor is nutrition education, so a block of time that otherwise might be allocated to these classes is used to meet reform requirements. Time is even reduced for school lunch to accommodate the focus on academics.

**The lack of physical activity and unhealthy eating are responsible for at least 300,000 preventable deaths each year in the United States.**

Costs are also a factor in the lack of P.E. Many school

systems do not have the funds to hire qualified P.E. teachers. Others do not have gyms or available space for gym classes.

"About two-thirds of young people in grades 9–12 are not engaged in recommended levels of physical activity," the CDC reported. "Daily participation in high school physical education classes dropped from 42 percent in 1991 to 33 percent in 2005."[7]

In June 2006, the federal government's *Morbidity and Mortality Weekly Report* published the results of its Youth Risk Behavior Surveillance System, which every other year since 1991 has monitored the top health-risk behaviors among youth and young adults. The risk behaviors include vehicle accidents, drug abuse, sexually transmitted diseases, unhealthy diets, and lack of physical activity. The report summarizes results of surveys conducted among students in public and private schools, grades 9–12, from October 2004 to January 2006.

According to the report, 9.6 percent of students in the nationwide assessment had not participated in any vigorous or moderate physical activity during the week before they were surveyed. The lack of activity was highest among females—11.3 percent compared to male inactivity at 7.9 percent. Inactive students often played video or computer games or used the computer for other than schoolwork more than three hours on the average school day. Nevertheless, 54 percent of surveyed students attended P.E. classes at least one day each school week, participating in exercise or sports. But *daily* participation in physical education was about 33 percent. A higher percentage of ninth graders attended P.E. class than tenth, eleventh, or twelfth graders, and overall males outnumbered females (60 percent to 48.3 percent) in P.E. attendance.

The report also noted that nearly 80 percent of students surveyed had not eaten the recommended servings of fruits and vegetables (five or more per day) during the seven days preceding the survey. A little more than 13 percent of students were overweight. More effective school health programs are needed to reduce risk and improve health among youth, the report advises.[8]

## Promoting Healthy Eating and Physical Activity

To counteract the health risks associated with inactivity, the CDC's Nutrition and Physical Activity Program developed KidsWalk-to-School. It is a community-based program that encourages children to walk or ride a bike short distances to and from school. The CDC states that only 16 percent of American children travel on foot or by bike to school. In contrast, several decades ago, the majority of students (90 percent) got to class by walking or biking.[9] The drop in the percentage of walkers and bicyclists is due to such factors as school consolidation (building large schools outside neighborhoods), heavy vehicle traffic, adverse weather conditions, fear of abductions, and neighborhood crime.

The KidsWalk program encourages civic leaders, parents, school personnel, police, and others to get involved and create safe routes for students. The program's goals include increasing awareness of the health benefits of regular physical activity and improving walkways, crosswalks, and bike paths so that students do not have to be driven or bused to school.

Along with federal agencies, educational associations, and the American Heart Association, the National Alliance for Nutrition and Activity (NANA) is a major promoter of physical education in schools. Its members represent more than three hundred organizations concerned about healthy living. One of NANA's primary goals is to promote children's health and well-being. Advocates urge the U.S. Congress and federal agencies to provide adequate funding for programs and environmental changes that help Americans eat better and be more active.

NANA also developed *Model School Wellness Policies on Physical Activity and Nutrition*, which school districts with federally funded meal programs were required to develop and put into operation by the start of the 2006–2007 school year. School districts may adapt the policies to fit their circumstances, but the model basically sets forth goals such as community involvement in school nutrition and physical activity efforts; opportunities for all students in grades K–12 to be physically active on a regular basis; access to a variety of affordable, nutritious, and appealing foods that meet the health and nutrition needs of students; and nutrition education and physical education to foster lifelong healthy habits.[10]

In some states, physical activity is being promoted by nontraditional means, such as "exertainment"—a term that combines "exercise" and "entertainment," coined by the audiovisual and video industry. One example is Dance Dance Revolution (DDR), a music-based video game, which has many variations. Players choose a song and operate the game with a dance pad that corresponds with four arrow panes pointing forward, back, left, and right on a screen. Watching the screen, players follow various sequences on the floor mat alone or with a partner. They can also engage in competitions.

In West Virginia, a state with a high rate of obesity, the Department of Education initiated a plan in 2006 to put DDR in all of its 765 public schools. It is the first statewide program to use the dance video game as a way to help reduce youth obesity. The program began with the recommendation of Linda M. Carson, distinguished professor at West Virginia University's School of Physical Education. She told a *New York Times* reporter that her inspiration came while

> in a mall walking by the arcade and I saw these kids playing D.D.R., and I was just stunned. There were all these kids dancing and sweating and actually standing in line and paying money to be physically active. And they were drinking water, not soda. It was a physical educator's dream.[11]

Other states using DDR in schools include California and

Hawaii. The game is also being used at some universities. At Brandeis University, for one, a DDR class is part of the physical education requirements for all students.

Skate In School is another nontraditional program encouraging student physical activity. It was developed by Rollerblade and the National Association of Sports and Physical Education. Schools purchase Rollerblade skates and protective gear (helmets and wrist, elbow, and knee guards) at reduced prices along with instruction for P.E. classes. The program is operating in schools across the country with an estimated one million students involved. "In-line skating is so cool that it doesn't even

**High schoolers play the video game Dance Dance Revolution as part of a program to increase student activity levels.**

feel like I'm getting exercise," one Los Angeles middle school student commented for the Rollerblade Web site. And a Boston high school student noted: "Skating is not just some team sport you only do at school. I can skate at home . . . and for the rest of my life."[12]

A variety of school clubs are also helping promote physical fitness among youth. There are unicycle clubs, for instance, that engage students in vigorous exercise on the unicycle on school playgrounds, tennis courts, or parking lots. School-sponsored skateboard and surfboard clubs are popular on the West Coast.

Obviously there are diverse ways to participate in physical activity. The point is to make it a regular part of one's daily life. The CDC recommends at least sixty minutes per day of moderate to vigorous physical activity for children and youth, although some experts suggest that ninety minutes of daily physical activity would be better. That time could be broken up into shorter periods that add up to an hour or more of individual sports, hiking, biking, swimming, dancing, P.E., gardening, or other physical tasks. It is a matter of using up calories and adding to the health benefits achieved through a nutritious eating plan.

If physical activities and nutritious eating become part of people's lives, does that mean they have to give up foods and beverages that they really like? Not at all, say dietitians and nutritionists. In the first place, a healthy diet does not consist of one set of specific foods and beverages. It can be imaginative and varied.

One teenager who put his imagination to work for healthy eating is Shawn DeMartino of Cape Cod, Massachusetts. Shawn started cooking and experimenting with recipes when he was only eleven years old. At the time he said he was overweight ("pudgy") and began exercising to slim down. Then he added healthy food to his regimen by cooking the evening meals for his family. One of his recipes is for a pizza with plenty of vegetables and boneless, skinless chicken breast. He also makes tacos with grilled fish—tilapia or mahi mahi—stuffed inside soft corn tortillas. He adds avocado salsa and shredded cabbage. For breakfast, he makes "mind blowing egg-white omelets," according to his father.[1]

"Through cooking, you learn to eat right," Shawn told a reporter. "And it stays with you for your whole life. If you start cooking as a kid, most times you keep those habits."[2] Shawn is hoping to launch a TV cooking show so that he can demonstrate how teens can create a healthy lifestyle.

## Teen Awareness

In a 2006 survey of more than five hundred teenagers, a marketing company found that most were aware that healthy eating is related to being in shape. A *Food Institute* report that published the survey noted that teenagers

> believe that what they eat has a direct relationship with ... their health and seek out products that can help them in their performance, whether it is in sports, weight or appearance. One way teenagers decide what to consume is through the categorization of what they're eating, into either "junk food" or "healthy food," with healthy food that doesn't sacrifice taste being the optimal choice. Approximately half of all teens, and more females than males, complain that health foods are too expensive, and there are not enough healthy snack options, when they do try and eat healthy, though nearly one-third felt food and drink companies do a good job producing new products that meet current health needs and trends.[3]

Teens may say they want healthy foods, but some of the most popular items that the respondents consumed were snacks—potato and tortilla chips and cookies, with fresh fruit the third option. A teenager in Boca Raton, Florida, was aware of this habit in her school. In *TeenInk*, she wrote that she "was disturbed by what I saw my peers eating—the majority ate lunch from the school's vending machines!" She pointed out that the vending machines contained "glazed honey buns, an assortment of candy bars, potato chips, soda, and similar snacks. I knew that to improve the health of students at my school, those machines needed an overhaul."

The Florida teenager began a campaign to change the snacks and other foods offered to students. At school, she distributed information on healthy food choices, spoke to elementary and middle school students around the state about healthy eating, and urged everyone to "vote with their forks." The slogan is from the film *Super Size Me*, in which filmmaker Morgan Spurlock documents his deteriorating health after thirty days of eating nothing but fast food from McDonald's. As the teenager put it: "We, as consumers, can make an impact on what is sold to us simply by making intelligent choices in what we decide to buy and eat."[4]

## Healthy Eating Habits

Most teens who want to develop healthy eating habits may begin by following the advice of numerous health experts: Start the morning by eating breakfast. Studies show that those who *do* eat breakfast have healthier body weights and better academic success than non-breakfast eaters. Eating breakfast also prevents the run-down feeling, the lack of energy that can occur midmorning because the body has insufficient fuel. By lunchtime a person may be not only hungry but also irritable and primed to eat nonnutritious, calorie-laden foods.

What is a healthy breakfast? One that contains protein (eggs, low-fat meat, or beans) and fiber such as whole-grain cereal and fruit. Another example is a vegetable omelet with a bran muffin and orange juice. A nutritious breakfast is even possible while eating on the go. One take-along is a whole-wheat pita stuffed with sliced hard-boiled eggs. Another is a

> **Teens who eat breakfast have healthier body weights and better academic success than non-breakfast eaters.**

bagel with peanut butter and some apple slices.

Healthy eating habits also include meals with the family, particularly dinner or supper. That may be difficult to establish, especially when some family members have after-school activities while others have evening work schedules or volunteer commitments. But a family meal does not have to be in the evening. It can occur whenever everyone can be together—breakfast, lunch, dinner, or even a regular snack time.

The importance of the eating together as a family has been underscored by a number of studies. One of them is Project EAT, which was conducted by researchers at the University of Minnesota. "The frequency of family meals during adolescence predicted higher intakes of fruit, vegetables, and key nutrients, as well as lower intakes of soft drinks during young adulthood," according to a press release and the study, published in the September 2007 *Journal of the American Dietetic Association.* "Frequent family meals during high school also predicted that the teens, as young adults, would eat breakfast and dinner meals more frequently, as well as place a high priority on meal structure and social eating."[5]

What about eating fast food at the family dinner table? Researchers concluded that the more families ate fast food at mealtime, the less fruits and vegetables they ate. They were also likely to have salty snacks and sugary soft drinks available. But no one suggested eliminating fast food altogether. Instead, it is a matter of limiting fast foods and adding more fruits, vegetables, whole grains, and low-fat milk.

## Ideas for Healthy and Enjoyable Eating

It has been said and written so often that it is like a mantra: Healthy eating means consuming fruits and vegetables, whole grains, unsaturated fats, and low-calorie foods and beverages. Are there simple ways to obtain these foods and still have an enjoyable eating experience?

Snacks made at home are a good way to start. Some examples include an apple with peanut butter, celery topped with peanut butter and raisins, trail mix, baby carrots and cherry tomatoes with a low-fat dip, or whole-grain crackers and string cheese.

Adding fruits and vegetables to one's diet can be as simple as mixing a whole-grain cereal with dried or fresh fruit or spreading a mashed banana or berries on whole wheat toast. You can also eat fruit for dessert, make a full meal of vegetable soup, drink a fruit smoothie or veggie quencher, or eat casseroles with more vegetables than meat or poultry.

It is a little more difficult to choose a healthy meal when you are eating out. But a few dos and don'ts may help:

- Do keep portions small.

- Do not supersize—try cutting a sandwich in half, for example.

- Do eat a lot of greens, especially salads with low-fat dressing.

- Do not load up salads or other foods with lots of cheese, croutons, or other "extras."

- Do eat grilled (rather than fried) meats, poultry, and fish.

- Do not habitually opt for fried, deep-fried, and breaded foods.

- Do drink low-calorie and low- or no-sugar beverages.

- Do not give up ALL foods that happen to be high in calories and saturated fat, but eat them sparingly.

**One way to improve your diet is to get involved in the creative process of preparing food.**

Finally, do not despair if you have not figured out all the healthy ways to eat. After all, nutritionists and dietitians spend years studying this topic, and research on healthful eating is ongoing. In short, there is no "perfect" eating plan. "No single food will make or break good health," wrote Dr. Willett of Harvard Medical School. "But the overall quality of your diet, the kinds of foods you choose to eat day in and day out, does have a major impact.... Enjoy food. But when push comes to shove, make choices that are high in flavor but also good for health."[6]

# Chapter Notes

### Chapter 1 Family, Friends, and Food

1. Jeffrey Kluger, Christine Gorman, and Alice Park, "Why We Eat," *Time*, June 7, 2004, <http://www.time.com/time/magazine/article/0,9171,994388,00.html> (October 4, 2007).

2. Brian Wansink, Ph.D., *Mindless Eating: Why We Eat More Than We Think* (New York: Bantam/Random House, 2006), p. 95–97.

3. National Center for Health Statistics, Centers for Disease Control and Prevention, "Prevalence of Overweight Among Children and Adolescents: United States, 2003–2004," January 30, 2007, <http://www.cdc.gov/nchs/products/pubs/pubd/hestats/overweight/overwght_child_03.htm> (April 25, 2008).

4. National Institute of Diabetes and Digestive and Kidney Diseases, National Institutes of Health, "Statistics Related to Overweight and Obesity," June 2007, <http://win.niddk.nih.gov/publications/PDFs/stat904z.pdf> (April 25, 2008).

5. "Defining Overweight and Obesity," Department of Health and Human Services, Centers for Disease Control and Prevention, May 22, 2007, <http://www.cdc.gov/nccdphp/dnpa/obesity/defining.htm> (April 25, 2008).

6. James R. Wallace, M.D., William J. Schulte, M.D., Atilla Nakeeb, M.D, Deborah A. Andris, APNP, "Health Problems Related to Severe Obesity," March 26, 2001, <http://healthlink.mcw.edu/article/984434798.html> (April 24, 2008).

7. National Center for Health Statistics and National Center for Chronic Disease Prevention and Health Promotion, 2000, <http://www.cdc.gov/growthcharts> (September 3, 2008).

8. Allison Guthrie, "Poor Nutrition in Teens," *Teen Voices*, May 2007, <http://www.teenvoices.com/issue_current/tvhealth_1.html> (May 19, 2007).

### Chapter 2 Junk Food, Fast Food, Smart Food

1. "Nearly One-third of the Calories in the US Diet Comprised of

Junk Food, Researcher Finds," *Science Daily*, June 2, 2004, <http://www.sciencedaily.com/releases/2004/06/040602061143. htm> (May 7, 2008).

2. Elaine Magee, MPH, RD, "Junk-Food Facts," August 8, 2007, <http://www.medicinenet.com/script/main/art.asp?articlekey= 56170> (April 24, 2008).

3. National Heart, Lung, and Blood Institute, "Frequent Fast Food Meals Increase Weight, Diabetes, Study Says," Press Release, December 30, 2004, <http://www.nih.gov/news/pr/dec2004/ nhlbi-30.htm> (October 5, 2007).

4. Dan Lippe, "Digital-Age Teen Eating Healthy—Sometimes," *Advertising Age*, January 2, 2006, p. 15.

5. Hope S. Warshaw, *Guide to Healthy Fast-Food Eating* (Alexandria, Va.: American Diabetes Association, 2006), p. 179.

6. See Web sites for Burger King, <http://www.bk.com/Nutrition/ PDFs/brochure.pdf>; KFC, <http://www.yum.com/nutrition/ documents/kfc_nutrition.pdf>; Subway, <http://subway.com/ subwayroot/MenuNutrition/Nutrition/pdf/NutritionValues.pdf>; and McDonald's, <http://app.mcdonalds.com/countries/usa/food/ nutrition/categories/nutritionfacts.pdf>.

7. U.S. Department of Health and Human Services, Centers for Disease Control and Prevention, "Physical Activity and Good Nutrition Essential Elements to Prevent Chronic Diseases and Obesity 2007," January 2007, <http://www.cdc.gov/nccdphp/ publications/aag/dnpa.htm> (October 5, 2007).

8. National Institute of General Medical Sciences, National Institutes of Health, *The Structures of Life*, Chapter 1, revised 2007, <http://publications.nigms.nih.gov/structlife/chapter1.html> (April 28, 2008).

9. Harvard School of Public Health, "Fats and Cholesterol—The Good, The Bad, and The Healthy Diet," n.d., <http://www.hsph. harvard.edu/nutritionsource/fats.html> (October 5, 2007).

10. "Questions and Answers about Trans Fat Nutrition Labeling," U.S. Food and Drug Administration, Center for Food Safety and

Applied Nutrition, January 1, 2006, <http://www.cfsan.fda.gov/ ~dms/qatrans2.html#s1q1> (October 5, 2007).

11. Miranda S. Spivack, "Montgomery Bans Trans Fats in Restaurants, Markets," *Washington Post*, May 16, 2007, p. A1.

12. Dave Carpenrter, "McDonald's cooking fries in trans-fat-free oil," *chicagotribune.com*, May 22, 2008, <www.chicagotribute.com/ business/chi-ap-mcdonalds-oil,0,3980585.story> (August 12, 2008.)

13. Adam Voiland, "No License to Overindulge," *U.S. News & World Report*, June 18, 2007, p. 58.

14. *MedlinePlus Health Information*, National Library of Medicine and the National Institutes of Health, November 1, 2006, <http://www. nlm.nih.gov/medlineplus/druginfo/natural/patient-fishoil.html> (October 5, 2007).

15. American Heart Association, "Fish and Omega-3 Fatty Acids," n.d., <http://www.americanheart.org/presenter.jhtml?identifier= 4632> (October 5, 2007).

16. U.S. Environmental Protection Agency, "What You Need to Know about Mercury in Fish and Shellfish," March 13, 2008, <http://www.epa.gov/waterscience/fish/advice/> (April 26, 2008).

## Chapter 3 Why and How We Eat

1. Kelly D. Brownell and Katherine Battle Horgen, *Food Fight: The Inside Story of the Food Industry, America's Obesity Crisis, and What We Can Do About It* (New York: McGraw-Hill/Contemporary Books, 2004), p. 21.

2. David Cameron, "Obesity Spreads through Social Networks," Harvard Medical School Office of Public Affairs, July 26, 2007, <http://web.med.harvard.edu/sites/RELEASES/html/ July07Christakis.html> (October 5, 2007).

3. Ibid.

4. Gina Kolata, "Find Yourself Packing It On? Blame Friends," *New York Times*, July 26, 2007, <http://www.nytimes.com/2007/07/26/ health/26fat.html?ex=1186286400&en=518926e6eb95cafa&ei= 5070> (October 5, 2007).

5. Kadesha McCastle, "Unhealthy Eating Habits," *Youth Radio Atlanta*, October 7, 2006, <http://www.youthradio.org/health/wabe061007_badfoods.shtml> (October 5, 2007).

6. Denae Bybee, "Young Girl Fights Obesity and Tells of Her Struggles," *BYU (Brigham Young University) NewsNet*, August 4, 2007, <http://newsnet.byu.edu/story.cfm/65002> (October 5, 2007).

7. American Heart Association, "Eating Breakfast May Reduce Risk Of Obesity, Diabetes, Heart Disease," *Journal Report*, March 6, 2003, <http://www.americanheart.org/presenter.jhtml?identifier=300971> (August 13, 2007).

8. Dorothy Rosenbaum, Center on Budget and Policy Priorities, "Families' Food Stamp Benefits Purchase Less Each Year," March 9, 2007, <http://www.cbpp.org/3-6-07fa.htm> (April 29, 2008).

## Chapter 4 Effects of Unhealthy Eating

1. Eve Conant, "Tele-Tubbies," *Newsweek.com*, March 28, 2007, <http://www.msnbc.msn.com/id/17838488/site/newsweek> (October 5, 2007).

2. The Henry J. Kaiser Family Foundation, *Food for Thought: Television Food Advertising to Children in the United States*, March 2007, <http://www.kff.org/entmedia/upload/7618.pdf> (August 17, 2007).

3. Ibid.

4. "Childhood Obesity Indicates Greater Risk Of School Absenteeism, Penn Study Reveals," University of Pennsylvania Press Release, August 10, 2007, <http://www.eurekalert.org/pub_releases/2007-08/uop-coi081007.php> (October 5, 2007).

5. "Obesity Rates Continue to Climb in the United States," Johns Hopkins School of Public Health, Press Release, July 10, 2007, <http://www.jhsph.edu/publichealthnews/press_releases/2007/wang_adult_obesity.html> (October 5, 2007).

6. U.S. Department of Health and Human Services, "Overview of Diabetes in Children and Adolescents, A Fact Sheet from the National Diabetes Education Program," August 2006, <http://

ndep.nih.gov/diabetes/pubs/Youth_FactSheet.pdf> (October 5, 2007).

7. American Diabetes Association, "Diabetes Myths," n.d., <http://www.diabetes.org/diabetes-myths.jsp> (April 30, 2008).

8. Ibid.

9. Sara Dabney Tisdale, "A Healthy Diet Promotes Healthy Lungs," *U.S. News & World Report,* July 9, 2007, <http://health.usnews.com/usnews/health/articles/070709/9asthma.htm> (October 5, 2007).

## Chapter 5 Eating Disorders

1. MedlinePlus Health Information, "Eating Disorder—Anorexia," May 21, 2007, <http://www.nlm.nih.gov/medlineplus/ency/article/000362.htm> (October 5, 2007).

2. MedlinePlus Health Information, "Bulimia nervosa; Binge-Purge Behavior; Eating Disorder—Bulimia," October 31, 2006, <http://www.nlm.nih.gov/medlineplus/ency/article/000341.htm> (October 5, 2007).

3. Ron Saxen, *The Good Eater: The True Story of One Man's Struggle with Binge Eating Disorder* (Oakland, Calif.: New Harbinger Publications, 2007), p. 3.

4. National Institute of Mental Health, *Eating Disorders: What Are Eating Disorders?*, February 17, 2006, <http://www.nimh.nih.gov/publicat/eatingdisorders.cfm> (October 5, 2007).

5. Substance Abuse and Mental Health Services Administration, "Eating Disorders," April 2003, <http://mentalhealth.samhsa.gov/publications/allpubs/ken98-0047/default.asp#2> (October 5, 2007).

6. McLean Hospital, "First National Survey on Eating Disorders Finds Binge Eating More Common Than Other Eating Disorders," Press Release, February 1, 2007, <http://www.mclean.harvard.edu/news/press/current.php?id=103> (October 5, 2007).

7. House Committee on Ways and Means, "Statement of National Association of Anorexia Nervosa and Associated Disorders," March

27, 2007, <http://waysandmeans.house.gov/hearings.asp?formmode=view&id=5932> (October 5, 2007).

8. Anorexia Nervosa and Related Eating Disorders, Inc., "What Causes Eating Disorders?" January 7, 2007, <http://www.anred.com/causes.html> (October 4, 2007).

9. Sandy Fertman Ryan, "Dying To Be Thin," *Girls' Life*, February–March, 2007, p. 52.

10. Anorexia Nervosa and Related Eating Disorders, Inc., "Statistics: How Many People Have Eating Disorders?" April 1, 2008, <http://www.anred.com/stats.html> (May 4, 2008).

11. National Eating Disorders Association, "Anorexia Nervosa," n.d., <http://www.edap.org/p.asp?WebPage_ID=286&Profile_ID=41142> (May 4, 2008).

12. McLean Hospital.

## Chapter 6 Healthy Eating

1. U.S. Department of Health and Human Services and the Department of Agriculture, *Dietary Guidelines for Americans*, 2005, p. vi, <http://www.health.gov/dietaryguidelines/dga2005/document/pdf/DGA2005.pdf> (October 5, 2007).

2. MyPyramid.gov, n.d., <http://www.mypyramid.gov/> (June 5, 2008).

3. Sally Squires, "Panel Urges Schools To Replace Junk Foods," *Washington Post*, April 26, 2007, p. A03.

4. Thomas C. Tobin, "Pinellas Earns an 'A' in Lunch," *St. Petersburg Times*, August 14, 2007, pp. B1, B6.

5. Daniel Shapiro, "Area Schools Serve Up Healthy Lunches," *Herald News NorthJersey.com*, January 28, 2007, <http://www.northjersey.com/page.php?qstr=eXJpcnk3ZjczN2Y3dnFlZUVFeXkzNTcmZmdiZWw3Zjd2cWVlRUV5eTcwNjc2NDImeXJpcnk3ZjcxN2Y3dnFlZUVFeXk0> (October 5, 2007).

6. Connecticut Climate Change, "At UConn, Local Routes Lead to Connecticut Farms," n.d., <http://www.ctclimatechange.com/documents/AtUConnLocalRoutesLeadtoCTFarms_000.pdf> (May 5, 2008).

7. "Food Certification Program," American Heart Association, n.d., <http://heartcheckmark.org/presenter.jhtml?identifier=2115> (October 5, 2007).

8. "Congressional Food Stamp Challenge," June 2007, <http://foodstampchallenge.typepad.com/> (October 5, 2007).

9. "Guidelines for Responsible Food Marketing to Children," Center for Science in the Public Interest, 2005, <http://www.cspinet.org/marketingguidelines.pdf> (October 5, 2007).

10. Andrew Martin, "Leading Makers Agree to Put Limits on Junk Food Advertising Directed at Children," *New York Times*, November 15, 2006, <http://www.nytimes.com/2006/11/15/business/media/15children.html?ex=1188273600&en=73d121358f8864f0&ei=5070> (October 5, 2007).

## Chapter 7 Weight-Loss Diets and Pills

1. Patricia van den Berg, Dianne Neumark-Sztainer, Peter J. Hannan, and Jess Haines, "Is Dieting Advice From Magazines Helpful or Harmful? Five-Year Associations With Weight-Control Behaviors and Psychological Outcomes in Adolescents," *Pediatrics Official Journal of the American Academy of Pediatrics*, Abstract, January 1, 2007, p. e30, <http://pediatrics.aappublications.org/cgi/content/abstract/119/1/e30> (October 5, 2007).

2. American Heart Association, "Quick-Weight-Loss or Fad Diets," n.d., <http://www.americanheart.org/presenter.jhtml?identifier=4584> (May 10, 2008).

3. Mayo Clinic Staff, "Detox Diets: Do They Offer Any Health Benefits?" April 11, 2006, <http://www.mayoclinic.com/health/detox-diets/AN01334> (May 8, 2008).

4. Ibid.

5. U.S. Department of Health and Human Services, Weight-control Information Network (WIN), "Diet Myths," fact sheet, August 2006, <http://win.niddk.nih.gov/publications/myths.htm#dietmyths> (October 5, 2007).

6. University of Minnesota News Service, "Use of Diet Pills By Teen Girls Nearly Doubles," Press Release, November 7, 2006, <http://

www1.umn.edu/umnnews/Feature_Stories/Use_of_diet_pills_by_teen_girls_nearly_doubles.html> (October 5, 2007).

7. U.S. Food and Drug Administration, "Dietary Supplements," October 5, 2007, <http://www.cfsan.fda.gov/~dms/supplmnt.html> (May 8, 2008).

8. Mayo Clinic Health Staff, "Over-the-counter weight-loss pills: Do they work?" May 31, 2007, <http://www.mayoclinic.com/health/weight-loss/HQ01160> (May 8, 2008).

9. Ibid.

10. Cable News Network, "Diet Pill Marketers Hit With False Ad Fines," January 4, 2007, <http://money.cnn.com/2007/01/04/news/companies/ftc_pills/index.htm> (October 5, 2007).

11. "You're Likely To Order More Calories At A 'Healthy' Restaurant," *Science Daily*, September 5, 2007, <http://www.sciencedaily.com/releases/2007/08/070829143638.htm> (May 7, 2008).

12. Public Citizen, "New York City's Fast-Food Calorie Labeling Rule Should Be Upheld, Groups Urge Federal Court," Press Release, July 16, 2007, <http://www.citizen.org/pressroom/release.cfm?ID=2476> (October 5, 2007).

13. U.S. Department of Health and Human Services, Weight-control Information Network (WIN), "Just Enough for You—About Food Portions," August 2006, <http://win.niddk.nih.gov/publications/just_enough.htm> (May 8, 2008).

**Chapter** 8 **Choosing the Vegetarian Way**

1. American Heart Association, "Vegetarian Diets," n.d., <http://www.americanheart.org/presenter.jhtml?identifier=4777> (October 5, 2007).

2. Laurie Dunham and Linda M. Kollar, "Vegetarian Eating for Children and Adolescents," Abstract and Introduction, *Journal of Pediatric Health Care, Medscape*, January 23, 2006, <http://www.medscape.com/viewarticle/521903> (September 2, 2007).

3. "Position of the American Dietetic Association and Dieticians of Canada: Vegetarian Diets," *Journal of the American Dietetic Association*, June 2003, p. 748.

4. "Our Mission," Christian Vegetarian Association, 2005, <http://www.all-creatures.org/cva/mission.htm> (October 5, 2007).

## Chapter 9 Physical Activity and Nutrition

1. NEA Health Information Network, "Physical Activity and Nutrition: School Children," 2005, <http://www.neahin.org/programs/physical/schoolchildren.htm> (May 9, 2008).

2. Ibid.

3. National Conference of State Legislatures, "Physical Activity and Nutrition," November 2003, <http://www.ncsl.org/programs/health/phyact.htm> (May 9, 2008).

4. Dawn Podulkam Coe, James M. Pivarnik, Christopher J. Womack, Mathew J. Reeves, and Robert M. Malina, "Effect of Physical Education and Activity Levels on Academic Achievement in Children," *Medicine & Science in Sports & Exercise*, August 2006, p. 38.

5. "Physical Activity and Fitness," Healthy People 2010, November 2000, <http://www.healthypeople.gov/Document/HTML/Volume2/22Physical.htm#_Toc490380803> (May 9, 2008).

6. National Association for Sport and Physical Education and the American Heart Association, Shape of the Nation Report: Status of Physical Education in the USA, Press Release, May 2006, <http://www.aahperd.org/naspe/ShapeOfTheNation/template.cfm?template=pressRelease.html> (October 5, 2007).

7. U.S. Department of Health and Human Services, Centers for Disease Control and Prevention, "Physical Activity and Health: Adolescents and Young Adults," November 17, 1999, <http://www.cdc.gov/nccdphp/sgr/adoles.htm> (May 9, 2008).

8. U.S. Department of Health and Human Services, Centers for Disease Control and Prevention, *Youth Risk Behavior Surveillance—United States*, 2005, <http://www.cdc.gov/mmwr/PDF/SS/SS5505.pdf> (May 9, 2008).

9. Centers for Disease Control and Prevention, KidsWalk-to-School, "Then and Now—Barriers and Solutions," n.d., <http://www.cdc.

gov/nccdphp/dnpa/kidswalk/then_and_now.htm> (October 5, 2007).

10. Model School Wellness Policies, n.d., <http://www. schoolwellnesspolicies.org/WellnessPolicies.html> (October 5, 2007).

11. Seth Schiesel, "P.E. Classes Turn to Video Game That Works Legs, Not Thumbs," *New York Times*, April 30, 2007, p. A1.

12. Rollerblade, "Skate in School Testimonials," n.d., <http://www. skateinschool.com/testimonials.htm> (October 5, 2007).

## **Chapter** 10 **Eating for Health and Enjoyment**

1. Jonathan Levitt, "Local Teen Hopes Smart Food Choices Bring TV Stardom," *Boston.com*, September 12, 2007, <http://www.boston. com/ae/food/articles/2007/09/12/local_teen_hopes_smart_food_ choices_bring_tv_stardom?mode=PF> (May 10, 2008).

2. Gwenn Friss, "Healthy Eating on Cape Teen's Menu," *Cape Cod Times*, September 5, 2007, <http://www.capecodonline.com/apps/ pbcs.dll/article?AID=/20070905/LIFE/709050301> (May 9, 2008).

3. "For Teens, Health Drives Food Consumption," *The Food Institute Report*, January 9, 2006, p. 1.

4. Arielle C., "Healthy Eating," *TeenInk*, December 2005, <http:// www.teenink.com/Poetry/article.php?link=Past/2005/December/ 19597.xml> (May 9, 2008).

5. University of Minnesota Academic Health Center, "U of M Research Finds Dietary Habits of Young Adults are Positively Influenced by Family Meals During High School," Press Release, August 20, 2007, <http://www.ahc.umn.edu/news/releases/ diet083007/home.html> (October 5, 2007).

6. Walter C. Willett, *Eat, Drink, and Be Healthy* (New York: Simon & Schuster, 2001), p. 192.

# Glossary

**amino acids**—Strings of molecules that form proteins.

**anorexia nervosa**—An eating disorder in which a person does not stay at the minimum body weight considered normal for his or her age and height.

**binge eating**—An eating disorder in which a person has recurrent episodes of significant overeating without purging.

**body mass index (BMI)**—The most commonly used method of calculating underweight and overweight; the ratio of the weight of the body to the square of its height.

**brewer's yeast**—A nutritional yeast that is a good source of B vitamins.

**bulimia nervosa**—An eating disorder in which a person has recurrent episodes of significant overeating followed by purging.

**carbohydrates**—Nutrients made up of carbon, oxygen, and hydrogen that combine to form sugar molecules; provide most of the energy our bodies need.

**cholesterol**—A soft, waxy substance produced by the body and obtained from food; combines with protein and fatty acids to form LDL ("bad" cholesterol) and HDL ("good" cholesterol).

**detox diets**—Diets that combine fasting with an extremely limited list of foods for a period in order to rid the body of toxins.

**diabetes**—A disease in which the body does not produce insulin (Type 1 diabetes) or does not use insulin properly (Type 2 diabetes).

**diabulimia**—An eating disorder among Type 1 diabetics who try to lose weight by not taking their insulin.

**eating disorder (ED)**—A psychological condition that includes a distorted view of self and extreme disturbances in eating behavior.

**ephedra (ma huang)**—A chemical used in some weight-loss aids, banned in the United States, that can cause serious health complications.

**fats**—Nutrients made up of fatty acids.

**kefir**—A cultured milk product similar to liquid yogurt.

**lacto-ovo vegetarian**—A person who eats no meat or fish, but does eat eggs and dairy products.

**miso**—A fermented soybean paste.

**morbid obesity**—A medical condition in which a person is a hundred pounds or more over the ideal body weight.

**obesity**—A condition in which a person has an abnormally high proportion of body fat.

**proteins**—Nutrients that build and repair body tissues and form antibodies to fight infections. Proteins are made from strings of molecules called amino acids.

**purging**—Ridding the body of food through such methods as vomiting or laxative abuse.

**tempeh**—A meat substitute made from soybeans.

**tofu**—A curd made from soybean milk.

**trans fat**—A type of fat that occurs naturally in small amounts in food; also formed when hydrogen is added to vegetable oil to make solid fat.

**vegan**—A person who eats no animal products.

# For More Information

American Diabetes Association
1701 North Beauregard Street
Alexandria, VA 22311
Phone: 800–342–2383

American Dietetic Association
120 South Riverside Plaza,
Suite 2000
Chicago, IL 60606-6995
Phone: 800–877–1600

American Heart Association
National Center
7272 Greenville Avenue
Dallas, TX 75231
Phone: 800–242–8721

American Obesity Association
8630 Fenton Street, Suite 814
Silver Spring, MD 20910
Phone: 301–563–6526

Centers for Disease Control
and Prevention
BMI Calculator
1600 Clifton Road
Atlanta, GA 30333
Phone: 800–232–4636

National Association of
Anorexia Nervosa and
Associated Disorders
P.O. Box 7
Highland Park, IL 60035
Phone: 847–831–3438

National Eating Disorders
Association
603 Stewart Street, Suite 803
Seattle, WA 98101
Phone: 800–931–2237

U.S. Department of Health and
Human Services
200 Independence Ave., SW
Washington, DC 20201
Phone: 877–696–6775

U.S. Food and Drug
Administration
5600 Fishers Lane
Rockville, MD 20857-0001
Phone: 888–463–6332

# Further Reading

Favor, Lesli J. *Food as Foe: Nutrition and Eating Disorders.* New York: Marshall Cavendish Benchmark, 2007.

Petri, Kristin. *Nutrition Anyone?* Edina, Minn.: Abdo Publishing Company, 2004.

Schlosser, Eric and Charles Wilson. *Chew on This: Everything You Don't Want to Know About Fast Food.* Boston: Houghton Mifflin, 2006.

Shryer, Donna. *Body Fuel: A Guide to Good Nutrition.* New York: Marshall Cavendish Benchmark, 2007.

Smolin, Lori A. and Mary B. Grosvenor. *Eating Right: an Introduction to Human Nutrition.* Philadelphia: Chelsea House, 2005.

U.S. Department of Health and Human Services and U.S. Department of Agriculture. *Dietary Guidelines for Americans, 2005.* Washington, D.C.: U.S. Government Printing Office, 2006.

Warshaw, Hope S. *Guide to Healthy Fast-Food Eating.* Alexandria, Va.: American Diabetes Association, 2006.

Williams, Kara. *Frequently Asked Questions About MyPyramid: Eating Right.* New York: Rosen Publishing Group, 2007.

# Internet Addresses

### American Heart Association—for Kids

<http://www.americanheart.org>

Click on "Children's Health," then "For Kids" on left side of page.

### Harvard School of Public Health Food Pyramids

<http://www.hsph.harvard.edu/nutritionsource/what-should-you-eat/pyramid/index.html>

### Medline Plus Health Information

<http://www.nlm.nih.gov/medlineplus>

### U.S. Department of Agriculture—Food Pyramid

<http://www.mypyramid.gov>

# Index